WHAT ANIMALS WANT

The Five Freedoms in Action

ORCA
Think

Question, connect and take action to become better citizens
with a brighter future. Now that's smart thinking!

WHAT ANIMALS WANT

The Five Freedoms in Action

Jacqueline Pearce

illustrated by Julie McLaughlin

ORCA BOOK PUBLISHERS

Originally published in Canada and the United States in 2021 by Orca Book Publishers.
This edition published for the BC SPCA (ISBN 9781459834309).
orcabook.com

Library and Archives Canada Cataloguing in Publication
Title: What animals want : the five freedoms in action / Jacqueline Pearce ; illustrated by Julie McLaughlin.
Names: Pearce, Jacqueline, 1962– author. | McLaughlin, Julie, 1984– illustrator.
Description: Series statement: Orca think; 3 | Includes bibliographical references and index.
Identifiers: Canadiana (print) 20210096470 | Canadiana (ebook) 20210096683 |
ISBN 9781459825659 (hardcover) | ISBN 9781459825666 (PDF) | ISBN 9781459825673 (EPUB)
Subjects: LCSH: Animal welfare—Juvenile literature.
Classification: LCC HV4708 .P43 2021 | DDC j636.08/32—dc23

Library of Congress Control Number: 2020951481

Summary: Part of the nonfiction Orca Think series, this book gives young readers the tools to think about the physical, social and emotional needs of pets, farm animals and wild animals using the Five Freedoms.

Orca Book Publishers is committed to reducing the consumption of nonrenewable resources in the making of our books. We make every effort to use materials that support a sustainable future.

Orca Book Publishers gratefully acknowledges the support for its publishing programs provided by the following agencies: the Government of Canada, the Canada Council for the Arts and the Province of British Columbia through the BC Arts Council and the Book Publishing Tax Credit.

Cover and interior artwork by Julie McLaughlin
Edited by Kirstie Hudson
Design by Rachel Page

Printed and bound in South Korea.

24 23 22 21 • 1 2 3 4

*For everyone who
dares to care*

A note about language:
The words we choose can make a difference in how we think about the things we're
talking about. We generally use the pronoun *that* to talk about objects—like a chair or
a hat—and *who* to refer to people. But how do we refer to animals? In this book, I've
chosen to use *who* instead of *that*, because animals are living beings who think, feel and
make choices—just like people do. I've also alternated between the male and female
pronouns he, she, him and her, rather than using the gender-neutral *it*.

Contents

INTRODUCTION

Have you ever walked a dog, petted a cat or fed a carrot to a guinea pig? Maybe you've ridden a horse or milked a cow. Perhaps you've seen **exotic** animals like elephants or tigers in a zoo, or tropical fish in an aquarium. Maybe you've heard an owl hoot or watched bats chasing bugs across the summer sky. Animals can be good company and fun to watch. Whether they live in our homes, our cities, on farms or in forests, deserts or oceans, animals are an important part of our world. And they make it a more interesting place to live. If you're like me, you care about your family and your community. You want everyone to have a good, happy, healthy life. And that means animals too.

When I was about 10 years old, a stray kitten wandered into our yard and made herself at home. From that time on, animals have been important to me—from pet cats, dogs, gerbils, guinea pigs and even a couple of rats to the wild birds, squirrels and coyotes who share my city. A tail wag from a friendly dog always raises my spirits. So does the song of a wild bird or the face of a raccoon peering down

Animals are an important part of our lives.
MARIECLAUDELEMAY/GETTY IMAGES

Ancient rock paintings, like these ones in Loy Canyon, AZ, show the close relationships people have had with animals for millennia.

DID YOU KNOW?

The Five Freedoms Checklist

- ☑ Freedom from hunger and thirst
- ☑ Freedom from pain, injury and disease
- ☑ Freedom from distress
- ☑ Freedom from discomfort
- ☑ Freedom to express behaviors that promote well-being

from a tree. The world would be a lonely place without the nonhuman animals around us.

For thousands of years, people have relied on animals—for food, clothing, help and companionship. Animals have provided meat, milk, fur and wool. They've guarded people's homes, helped with hunting and herded sheep. They've pulled plows, wagons and sleds, and they've carried people and belongings on their backs. They have also been loyal, loving companions. Animals have been part of our stories and myths going back to the earliest times, when our ancestors painted images of them on the walls of caves. Today animals play major roles in some of our most loved books and movies, from *Peter Rabbit* to *The Lion King*.

Yet people haven't always treated animals kindly.

How people act toward animals has varied at different times in history and in different places around the world. In some places in the past, people considered animals important and magical. In other times and places, people valued animals only for their usefulness. As societies change and awareness grows, attitudes and behaviors also shift. Today pets are part of many people's families, and most societies around the world believe that people have a responsibility to take good care of the animals we live with. This includes pets, farm animals, zoo animals and our wild animal neighbors.

Since animals can't tell us how they feel or what they want, sometimes it's hard to know if their lives are good or bad. Scientists who study animals can help us understand the biology, habits and needs of different animals, so that we can know if they are getting the right type of food, shelter, socialization, exercise and medical care. What is good for one animal is not always good for another.

Cats and dogs both like to eat meat, but cats actually need meat more than dogs do (find out why in chapter 1). Dogs like to play in wide outdoor spaces (sometimes with people and

TRUE OR FALSE?

It's against the law to hurt an animal.
This is true in many countries. The first *animal welfare* law was created in England in 1822. People were becoming concerned about the hard lives of working animals— especially horses in cities and ponies working underground in coal mines.

The world's first Society for the Prevention of Cruelty to Animals (SPCA) was formed in England in 1824. It was given royal status by Queen Victoria (who was an animal lover) and became known as the Royal Society for the Prevention of Cruelty to Animals (RSPCA). The American Society for the Prevention of Cruelty to Animals (ASPCA) was created in 1866. The first SPCA in Canada was started soon afterward.

Scientists are still learning about the complexity of animal needs.
CHENDONGSHAN/SHUTTERSTOCK.COM

All animals need to feel safe.
BC SPCA

other dogs), but a small animal like a rat or a gerbil needs a quiet place to hide. A large marine animal like an orca needs hundreds of miles of ocean to swim in. Every animal has physical needs. Now scientists are telling us that animals have social and emotional needs too. How do we know if an animal is happy and content or sad and stressed?

Back in 1965, animal scientists in the United Kingdom developed a tool called the Five Freedoms to help improve the treatment of animals raised in *factory farms*. The Five Freedoms checklist has since been applied to any animal kept under the care of people. Each "freedom" focuses on a different area of animal life. Together, they help people evaluate an animal's overall welfare. *Welfare* refers to how well an animal is doing physically and mentally. The Five Freedoms guidelines are now used around the world (sometimes with slightly different wording, but with the same main ideas). The version used in this book was developed by the British Columbia Society for the Prevention of Cruelty to Animals (BC SPCA).

It's a list that works for people too. No one wants to be hungry, thirsty, hurt or afraid. Right? But when someone can't talk, how can you tell if they're afraid, or uncomfortable, or sad, or happy, or hungry or bored? Can you tell by the expression on a person's face? Animals may not show their feelings the same way people do, but they do give clues. Learning about animals and their characteristics can help us understand what animals like and don't like. It can even help us understand what they are feeling. As you read through these pages, you'll find out how people (even kids) are using the Five Freedoms to help animals.

DID YOU KNOW?

Words to Know

Companion animals (also called pets) have been bred to live and thrive in relationships with humans.

Domesticated animals (which include pets and farm animals) have wild ancestors, but they have been bred by people over many generations (in some cases, thousands of years) to emphasize certain physical and behavioral traits, such as milk production in dairy cows, retriever skills in some dog breeds or lap size in others. These animals are now dependent on people to take care of them.

Exotic animals are wild animals who either have been taken from their natural habitats or bred while in captivity. They are purchased by individual people, zoos, aquariums or circuses, and they can end up far away from the natural habitat in which they are healthy and happy. Some countries have laws against selling and buying exotic-animal products or keeping exotic animals as pets.

Farm animals are raised on farms to provide food, products like wool or do work for people.

Habitat is the natural home of wild animals—where they eat, sleep and raise their young. Different animals have adapted to different habitats, such as forests, mountains, grasslands, deserts, oceans, lakes or rivers.

Humane means compassionate and kind. Treating animals humanely is to treat them with kindness and respect.

Welfare refers to the health, happiness and quality of life of an individual or group of animals.

Wild animals are part of a natural *ecosystem* and live separately from people. But some wild animals have adapted to living in cities and even build nests on buildings.

One
FOOD AND WATER FIRST!

Most of you take a lunch to school each day, including a bottle of water or a juice box. Some schools have a lunch program that provides food or a cafeteria where you can buy food. Like people, animals need food and water to survive. Wild animals have to **forage** for their food and water. Some animals, like shrews and hummingbirds, spend much of their day searching for food and snacking. Others, like lions, commonly eat only one big meal a day. A boa constrictor might eat one meal every week or two. Pets, farm and zoo animals rely on people to feed them.

WHAT'S ON THE MENU?

In the past, people didn't understand the nutritional needs of animals. They knew through observation that certain animals ate meat, while others ate plants or insects, but they didn't know why. And they didn't understand why one type of meat or vegetation was good for some animals and not for others.

Pet rats enjoy dry rat food, a variety of fresh fruit and veggies, plus fresh water to drink. Different animals have different food needs. BC SPCA

Both cats and dogs (and their wild relatives) enjoy eating meat, but their nutritional needs are not the same. Dogs are omnivores, which means they can eat both vegetables and meat, while cats are carnivores, which means meat is their main food. Cats need to eat taurine, which is an essential amino acid found in animal protein, such as meat and fish. Dogs and people need taurine too, but our bodies can make taurine, so we don't need to get it directly from our food. Cats' bodies can't produce enough taurine on their own. Taurine **deficiency** can cause eye problems and heart disease. Today, thanks to **veterinary** scientists who study cat nutrition, store-bought cat food is required to contain the taurine and other nutrients cats need to stay healthy.

Small pets like guinea pigs, gerbils and rabbits also have specific dietary needs. They enjoy a mix of store-bought

Cats need to eat food that has taurine in it, which includes meat, fish and store-bought cat food.
KSENIYA OVCHINNIKOVA/GETTY IMAGES

pellets, hay, fresh vegetables and the occasional piece of fruit. But what's good for a rabbit or gerbil might not be good for a guinea pig. Like people, guinea pigs need **vitamin C** in their diet, as without it they will get a disease called scurvy. Sailors used to get scurvy when they were out at sea for a long time and didn't eat enough fruit. It can cause weakness, swollen joints and bleeding. People get vitamin C from eating fruits and vegetables. Fresh fruit and vegetables, such as red peppers, kale, apples and parsley, are also good sources of vitamin C for guinea pigs. Timothy hay is another food that has vitamin C. Guinea pigs eat timothy hay to help with digestion. Vitamin C is added to pellets for guinea pigs, which is why you shouldn't feed rabbit pellets to guinea pigs. Pet-supply stores have a separate section for each type of animal to help you choose the right food and other supplies.

NO JUNK FOOD, PLEASE!

Foods that are high in sugar or fat, like candy, cake, soda pop, potato chips and fast-food fries and burgers, are unhealthy for people and pets. Sometimes people feed their dogs table

A healthy diet, which includes pellets with vitamin C, keeps guinea pigs happy.
ALEXANDRA JURSOVA/GETTY IMAGES

CARE TIP

Pet Food Homework
If you have a pet, or you're thinking of getting one, find out what food is right for that animal and what food is not. Search the internet. Look for trustworthy sources of information, such as the local SPCA, your veterinarian (vet) or specific animal-club websites. Pet-supply stores can usually offer good advice, but it's better to ask at your local vet clinic. Don't forget that the right amount of food is important to know too. Check the back of the food package for the correct amount to feed your pet, or ask your vet. You don't want your pet to go hungry, but you also don't want your pet to overeat.

scraps, but certain human foods are bad for pets. Oily and fatty foods can cause diarrhea, vomiting, stomach pain and serious health problems. Onions, raisins, grapes and chocolate are even toxic to dogs. Foods with bones or pits are also dangerous, because they can get stuck in a dog's throat or intestines.

Even when you're feeding the right food, you have to be careful not to give your pets too much, whether it's treats or their regular food. Like people, dogs and cats (and other pets) can put on extra weight and develop health issues associated with obesity—especially if they eat a lot and don't get enough exercise.

But food can also be fun. You can use high-value (extra-tasty) treats, such as little pieces of dehydrated chicken, cut-up wieners or cheese, to help train your dog to follow basic commands like "come" and "sit" or to reward your dog for returning a Frisbee or running an agility course. Rats can also be trained to jump through hoops and do other simple activities to get a treat. My two cats spend a lot of time sitting around, so I use treats to encourage them to get exercise. They love to chase their treats down our long hallway.

FOOD FOR THOUGHT

Many countries now have regulations (rules and laws) about providing farm animals and pets with good nutrition and fresh water at all times. But supplying food and water is not enough. You also need to make sure animals can actually *get* the food and water and that it's something they want to eat. I put out two dishes of food for my two cats, but one cat is a faster eater and is greedy. If I'm not watching, he'll push away the other cat and eat her food too, which means she won't get enough to eat. And if I try to give them a food they don't like, they will refuse to eat and keep meowing until I give them something they like.

Animals need not only the right food but also food they like and can get to.
SALLY ANSCOMBE/GETTY IMAGES

Cows like to graze on grass and other plants outdoors.
ANDRE WILMS / EYEEM/GETTY IMAGES

Farm animals, too, can prefer one food over another. Did you know that farmers often feed cattle grain but that too much grain can give them a stomachache? They would rather eat fresh grass, and their stomachs have four compartments, designed to break down and digest tough plants. In the wild, animals forage for food. Farm animals like to do this too. It's more interesting than eating out of a bowl or trough, and it gives them some healthy exercise.

Farm animals can also get pushed away from food by other animals or have problems getting their dinner and water if something blocks their way to it or it gets knocked over. Both farmers and pet guardians need to check that animals are getting to the food and water put out for them and that it's always fresh and clean.

If food is not stored properly, it can get damp and moldy. If water has been sitting around for a while, it can become contaminated with dirt, feces (poop), parasites or algae (plantlike organisms). Old food and water can stop tasting good, lose nutritional value and make animals sick. Even natural sources of water, such as ponds and streams for outdoor animals, need to be checked regularly. Sometimes agricultural chemicals or animal feces get into food or water and make animals sick. Sometimes water that is good in the winter is not drinkable in the summer.

WINTER WORRIES

Have you ever noticed that you feel hungrier in the winter than in the summer? Our bodies use more energy to keep warm in winter, so we need more fuel to give us that energy boost. The same is true for animals. During cold spells, farm animals need extra daily feed to stay strong and healthy.

Beef cattle, sheep and other animals kept outside need ice-free water. Some farmers and ranchers expect their animals to get water from snow, but drinking cold snow makes it even harder for animals to stay warm. Plus, the animals don't like it. On large ranches cattle often get their water from a pond, and the rancher needs to break the ice when temperatures drop below freezing.

Some farmers provide insulated drinking troughs to keep the water from freezing. Out on the range, solar-powered heaters are sometimes used. Other farms in North America (and a few in Europe) use a water pump that depends on cow

DID YOU KNOW?

Rats Have Taste Buds Too

Rats can be just as picky as people when it comes to food. They can tell the difference between foods that are salty, sweet, sour or bitter. Also like us, if rats like or dislike a food, they can show it through different facial expressions (kind of like making a "yum" or "yuck" face). A good sense of taste is important for rats, because in the wild anything is potential food, and rats need to find out whether something is safe to eat or not. They also learn and remember. If rats taste a flavor that's made them sick in the past, they leave it alone.

These cows are using their noses to pump drinking water from pipes buried under the ground to keep the water from freezing. FROSTFREE NOSEPUMPS LTD.

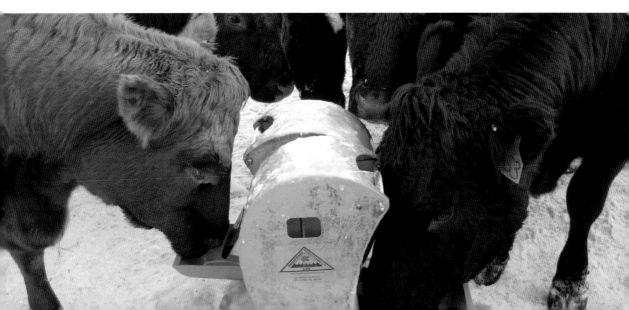

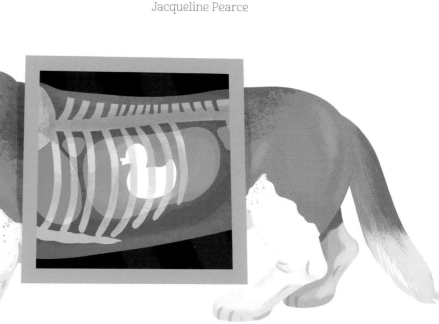

power. The water is kept in pipes deep enough underground that it can't freeze, and cattle push on a pump with their noses to bring water up to a drinking trough. The animals have to learn how to use the pump, but once a few catch on, they teach others. The pump also stops them from stepping in their water and polluting it. Cattle like to use the nose pump in summer, too, because it provides cool, clean water.

HOLIDAY SAFETY

Holidays such as Halloween, Christmas, Hanukkah and Chinese New Year, and special events like birthday parties, are all times when there is extra human food around and other dangers to pets. We've already mentioned some poison and choking hazards. Non-food items can also be dangerous if pets mistake them for food. Cats will often try to eat tinsel or ribbon, which can get stuck in their throats and intestines. Dogs have been known to steal food off people's plates and accidentally swallow candy wrappers, napkins and even knives and forks.

Bella needed emergency surgery to remove these seven rubber ducks she'd swallowed.
CATERS NEWS AGENCY

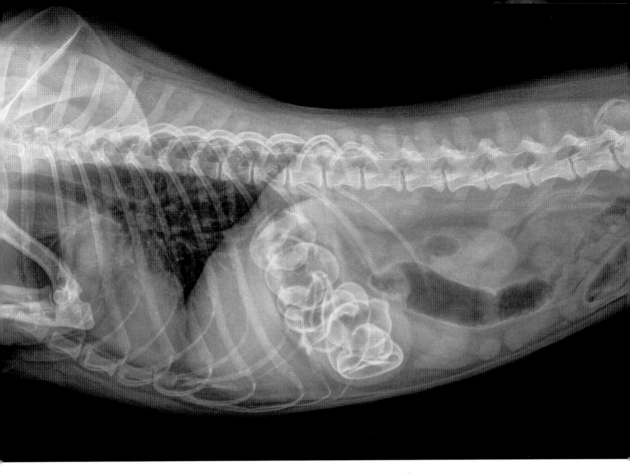

It's always good to keep an eye on pets around food and keep your own toys and small items out of the reach of pets. Some decorative plants displayed during these holidays, such as mistletoe and holly, are poisonous if eaten by pets. At other times of the year, be careful with plants such lilies, daffodils, tulips and tomatoes. Outside the house, pet guardians need to make sure their pets aren't eating or drinking poisons such as sweet-tasting liquid antifreeze (which keeps the water in car radiators from freezing) or de-icing salt and chemicals. Pets can also step in poisons like antifreeze or chemicals used on lawns in summer, then get sick when they lick their paws. Wiping paws is a good precaution.

Another thing to consider during holidays is that pets need a quiet, safe place to stay while guests come and go or when fireworks go off.

Can you spot the rubber ducks in Bella's X-ray?
CATERS NEWS AGENCY

Speaking Out Against Dangerous Antifreeze
When Justice Janveaux-Huolt was 11, the animal lover from Campbell River, BC, brought a petition to the provincial government. She collected more than a thousand signatures supporting a ban on ethylene glycol-based antifreeze, which kills thousands of animals each year. Her petition helped persuade the provincial government to order manufacturers to add a bitter taste to antifreeze to discourage pets, wildlife and children from drinking it, and require recycling centers to collect antifreeze. This doesn't stop toxic ethylene glycol from being used, but it makes a difference. Justice's action also drew public attention to the problem, and now more people are choosing to buy antifreeze made with propylene glycol, which is nontoxic.

BC SPCA

PLEASE DON'T FEED WILDLIFE

Did you know that feeding wild animals can be more harmful than helpful? It may cause wild animals like bears and raccoons to lose their fear of people, which is a safety concern for people *and* animals. It may also encourage animals to crowd around the food source, raising the risk of disease being spread, as well as fighting.

Sometimes people don't feed wildlife on purpose, but they leave out garbage cans or compost that animals can get into. Keeping your garbage cans inside a garage or shed or using secure lids that racoons and bears can't open helps keep your wild neighbors safe and healthy.

People love to feed bread to ducks and geese, but bread—especially white bread and similar foods such as crackers and donuts—fills birds up without giving them the nutrition they need. It can cause ducks, geese and swans to develop a condition known as "angel wing," which means their wings get deformed and they can't fly. It can also prevent ducklings and goslings from learning to forage for their own food. Wild ducks and geese can live longer, healthier lives if they stick to their natural diet of water plants, seeds, grasses and insects.

Similarly, when backyard birds eat too much bread or other human foods, their babies don't develop properly. They can end up with brittle bones that break easily. Adults will not have enough energy for annual migrations.

Does this mean you can never feed birds? Not exactly. It's okay to put out a backyard bird feeder in the winter when it's harder for birds to find wild food—as long as you put out fresh seed mix designed for wild birds and you clean the bird feeder regularly. Mold and bacteria can make birds sick. It also doesn't hurt to occasionally feed pond birds (where allowed) if you give them healthy treats like salad greens, fresh vegetables, whole-grain oats and seeds. You can usually find wild birdseed at a pet-supply or grocery store. When the temperature drops in winter, backyard birds and other wild creatures will also appreciate a dish or tray of clean, ice-free water.

TRUE OR FALSE?

Milk is not good for cats. Surprising, but true! Cats like the taste of milk, but cows' milk is actually not good for them. Kittens need to drink milk from their mother (all baby mammals need their mother's milk), but once they grow up, they don't need milk. And cows' milk is not designed for cats. In fact, most cats are **lactose intolerant**, so feeding them cows' milk can give them an upset stomach and other health issues. The best drink for your cat is water.

Backyard birds are happy to find a well-maintained feeder and unfrozen water in winter.
ROTOFRANK/GETTY IMAGES

Two

HEALTH MATTERS

When was the last time you went to the doctor for a checkup or had to take medicine when you were sick? Animals need health checks too. If they're injured or sick, they need to visit a veterinarian. Like people, animals also need **vaccinations** to prevent them from getting certain diseases. Freedom from pain, injury and disease means ensuring that animals get the medical care they need right away so they don't suffer.

THE HISTORY OF HEALING ANIMALS

Throughout much of human history, there have been healers who specialize in treating animals. Shepherds and farmers treated sick animals with herbs, helped pregnant animals deliver their babies and perhaps splinted broken bones. Ancient Egyptian tomb drawings show healers looking after cattle and assisting with the birth of calves more than 4000 years ago.

During the Middle Ages in Europe, farriers, who made iron shoes for horses, were also expected to know a bit about horse doctoring. As early as 1356, farriers in London, England,

Regular vet checkups help keep pets healthy. BC SPCA

KIDS IN ACTION

A Childhood Passion Becomes a Career
Caitlin McLagan's interest in helping animals started when she was a kid attending BC SPCA summer camps. She studied veterinary medicine in university and spent a month working with the Maun Animal Welfare Society in Botswana, where she traveled from village to village vaccinating and sterilizing local companion animals and providing other basic veterinary services. She also got to see some amazing animals, such as elephants and giraffes, in the wild.

BC SPCA

The ASPCA in New York City started the first ambulance for horses in 1867.

organized to help improve the care of horses in that city. The modern profession of veterinary medicine started with the founding of the first veterinary school in Lyon, France, in 1761. At that time, keeping an animal as a pet wasn't as common as it is today, so vets focused mainly on working horses and farm animals. It wasn't until modern times that pets became popular and people began taking their pets to vets for regular checkups.

In the middle of the 20th century (after World War II), average North American families began to have more income and could spend money on things that used to be considered "extras," including pets, store-bought pet food and vet bills. For the first time people were willing to spend money to fix a pet's broken bones and heal their diseases. Veterinary medicine was also becoming more popular in North America and other wealthier countries, and by the 1950s there were more vets than ever before. People realized they could take their animals to a "doctor"—not just when they were sick or injured, but for regular checkups and vaccinations too.

HOME HEALTH CHECKS

Besides taking your pet for vet visits (at least once a year is recommended—more often for senior pets), you can also do home health checks. Is your pet eating, drinking and pooping regularly? Is your pet's fur shiny and healthy? Ears clean and dry? Eyes clear and bright? Has your pet been scratching more than usual? Are there any sores or red patches on your pet's skin? Red patches and itching could be signs of allergies, fleas or infections. If your pet is limping, something might be stuck in your pet's paw, or there might be something more seriously wrong (like when my kitten had a broken leg). Just like you, cats, dogs and even rabbits need regular dental checkups and teeth cleaning—at least once a year.

Keeping an eye on pet and farm animals' nails, hooves, teeth and coats is also part of a home health check. In the wild, most animals' nails and hooves will wear down from natural activity, such as walking on hard ground, climbing on rocks and scratching tree bark. But pets and farm animals

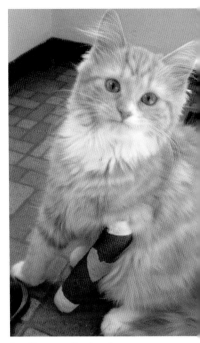

Our kitten was limping after roughhousing with her brother, so we took her to the vet. An X-ray revealed she had a broken leg and needed a cast.
J. PEARCE

Farm animals need health checks too.
MLADENBALINOVAC/GETTY IMAGES

often need their nails or hooves trimmed and their fur or coats groomed. Sheep need their wool sheared (cut) each spring or it will grow too long and possibly become tangled in bushes and fences.

Some animals can help with their own health checks. Dogs and horses can be taught to lift a paw or hoof and wait while it's checked over. Zoo workers have even trained giraffes to lift a foot for an X-ray or a blood sample. You can help your pets feel more comfortable with home health checks and vet visits, as well as with having their nails trimmed and their teeth brushed. Start by gently handling your pet's feet, ears and mouth and rewarding each time with a treat. This will help your pet associate these activities with something positive.

STOPPING THE SPREAD OF DISEASE

Just like you, all animals get sick from time to time. Most illnesses are not serious and can be easily treated—especially if the problem is caught quickly. Many farm-animal diseases can be treated with **antibiotics** or other medications. Some diseases can be prevented through vaccinations. But some illnesses are more serious, and they can spread from animal to animal, farm to farm and even country to country. As we know from human experience, when a sickness travels around the world, it's called a **pandemic**.

In the 1980s and 1990s, several countries experienced outbreaks of mad cow disease, a brain disease that killed thousands of cows. Farmers were ordered to kill thousands more to keep the illness from multiplying. In recent years there have also been outbreaks of bird flu, which moved through chicken farms and led to the death of millions of chickens and turkeys. That's why modern farmers do everything they can to stop the spread of disease.

This sick goat has been quarantined to keep disease from spreading.
JO-ANNE MCARTHUR/WE ANIMALS

CARE TIP

Giving a Pet Pedicure
Did you know that rabbits and guinea pigs need to get their nails done? You don't have to take them to a salon though. You just need the right set of nail clippers.

In the wild, the nails of guinea pigs and rabbits wear down naturally, but pet guinea pigs and rabbits need their nails clipped monthly, or they will just keep growing! Unclipped nails can end up curling under and poking into the animal's feet, making it painful and difficult to walk. Cats' and dogs' nails often wear down naturally through activities, but they may sometimes need their nails trimmed too.

Always be careful to cut above the quick (the pink part of the nail). Cutting too close to the quick can cause pain and bleeding.

BC SPCA

This sow and piglets in a farrowing crate are being checked by a vet who is "gowned up" to help prevent the spread of disease.
RAT0007/GETTY IMAGES

Keeping careful records means farmers know the history and movement of each animal (when animals are sold or transported from one location to another). Every visitor to a farm needs to log in, so that when a disease is spotted, it can be quickly traced to its source and action taken to stop the spread. Modern barns also follow bio security protocols (rules). Visitors are asked to gown up before entering a barn. That means putting on protective coveralls with a hood, wearing a dust mask and covering shoes with plastic booties. It's especially important to cover shoes, because one of the main ways diseases are transmitted from farm to farm is on the bottom of shoes.

NO GAIN FROM PAIN

Many routine farm procedures such as dehorning, **branding** and **castrating** (**neutering**) cattle are painful to animals. In the past these were considered acceptable practices, and people didn't realize how much suffering they caused. Dairy cows naturally grow horns. The horns can injure other cows or people, so farmers remove them when the cows are young. They do this by applying a hot iron or acid paste to the sensitive tissue on a calf's head where the horns will grow. Called disbudding, this stops the horns from growing. But recent science has shown that these procedures are extremely painful to the calves. If pain medication is given before and after, the calves don't suffer as much. Many countries now require farmers to use pain medication before and after disbudding, castration and branding. In fact, hot-iron branding is being replaced by freeze branding because it is less painful. More progressive farmers are moving to radio-frequency microchip tags, which are pain-free.

It also used to be common for some dog breeds to have their tails docked (shortened) and their ears cropped

This calf was given an injection for pain relief before acid paste was applied to prevent the young animal's horns from growing. BC SPCA

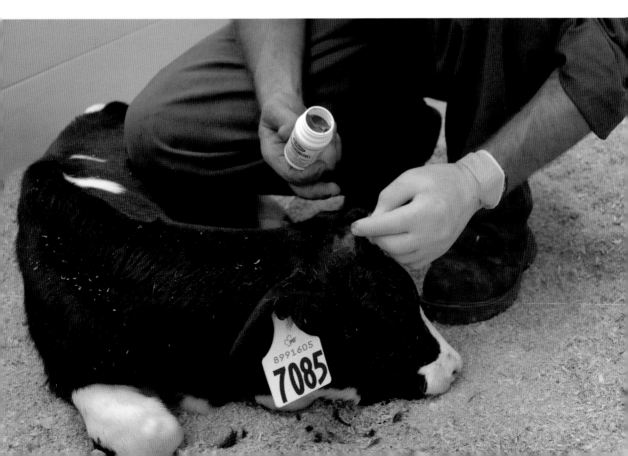

The young dog pictured here has had his ears cropped, bandaged and splinted, so that the ears will heal standing straight up. How do you think the dog feels? BC SPCA

This dog's ears have not been cropped. They can flop and move naturally, which is important in dog communication. BRIGHTON DOG PHOTOGRAPHY/GETTY IMAGES

(the floppy part of the ears cut off). This was done for "looks." Breeds such as Dobermans, boxers and schnauzers couldn't win dog shows if they didn't have their ears cropped and their tails docked. People thought that if the cutting was done when puppies were young, their **nervous systems** wouldn't be developed enough to feel pain. But science shows that puppies do feel pain (just as young calves do). Docking tails and cropping ears causes pain and can lead to emotional trauma and health risks.

Also, dogs use their tails and ears to convey information to other dogs (and people), so removing them makes it hard for dogs to communicate. Tail position can show friendliness, readiness to play, fear or a warning to stay away. Ears flat against the head may show fear or aggression. Today tail docking is banned in many countries, including Sweden, Denmark, Germany, Australia and the United Kingdom.

In several other places, including some American states and Canadian provinces, it is considered **unethical** by veterinary associations, and vets will not do the operation unless it's for a health reason.

Most people today understand that animals feel pain. If a dog hurts her paw, she whimpers. If a cat gets his tail stepped on, he yowls. Cows moo and learn to fear electric fences and prods (electrified sticks used to nudge an animal to move into a pen or onto a truck). Some animals don't make noises when they feel pain (especially if they've learned to stay quiet to keep hidden from predators), but they may show different facial expressions, grind their teeth, twitch their whiskers or nostrils, or show other physical changes.

Cows quickly learn that electric fences cause pain, and they try to keep away.
CASARSAGURU/GETTY IMAGES

Instead of dissecting frogs, science classes can use models and apps to learn about anatomy.
SOCIETY FOR HUMANE SCIENCE

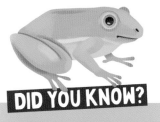

IT'S NOT EASY BEING GREEN

It's easy for most people to know through observation that animals such as chimpanzees, horses, dogs and cats feel pain. It's harder to tell whether creatures like frogs, fish and lobsters feel pain. Frogs were commonly used in experiments and **dissected** in school science labs. Recent studies, however, show that frogs and other amphibians possess neuro (nerve) pathways that allow them to feel pain. Frogs also move away from things that could hurt them, which indicates they feel pain and try to avoid it. If someone was poking you in the leg, you'd pull away too!

The knowledge that even a frog or a fish can feel pain is leading to changes in human behavior. When people work with animals on a farm or in a science lab, they can give them pain-relief medication or **anesthetics** to put them to sleep. Farmers and scientists can also look for alternatives to causing an animal pain, such as not cutting off cows' tails, or breeding polled cows (cows who don't grow horns in the first place). Animals used for food (such as that beef burger you might eat) can be killed humanely, with as little pain and stress as possible. Even lobsters can be stunned, or killed humanely, before they're dropped in boiling water.

Some people are choosing not to eat animals at all, becoming vegetarian or vegan. There are scientists exploring alternatives to using live animals in research. In some cases, they might be able to test new medicines, cosmetics or household products on cells grown in a lab instead of testing them on a live rabbit or other animal. Some high school science classes are replacing live frogs with plastic frog models or virtual dissection apps to teach students about the anatomy (body structure) of frogs. New virtual dissection apps are also better for learning and save money for schools. Plus, they make life a lot easier for frogs.

Many cats can be happy and healthier living indoors—especially if they have interesting places to play, climb and perch. W-INGS/GETTY IMAGES

TRUE OR FALSE?

Cats don't need to go outside.
This is true with most pet cats. They can be happy staying inside—especially if you have places for them to climb and good spots for them to lounge and look around. Cats who stay indoors may also be healthier. If they go outside, they are exposed to ticks and fleas, as well as diseases from other cats. They can get hit by cars or injured in fights with neighborhood cats and encounters with wild animals like raccoons and coyotes. It's safer for songbirds, too, if cats stay indoors. Outdoor cats injure and kill millions of birds each year, as well as other wildlife.

But if cats don't get enough exercise inside, they may get bored, become overweight and develop a disease called diabetes (this can happen to dogs too). That's one of the reasons it's important to play with your cat. Also remember that if you have more than one cat, each cat needs his or her own food and water dishes, litter box and places to climb and sit.

Three

STOP THE SUFFERING

Have you ever had a cut or a broken bone? Maybe you've missed a meal and been hungry, or eaten something that gave you a stomachache. These are all physical stresses on your body. Have you ever felt anxious or scared about taking a test? How about getting yelled at? These are emotional stresses. Luckily, stress usually doesn't last long, and you soon feel better. Like you, animals often cope with short-term stresses—they're part of life. But when physical or emotional stress becomes long-term, it can lead to distress (the continual state of stress). If the distress becomes life-threatening, it is considered critical distress, meaning the animal's life is in danger.

If an injury or sickness isn't treated, an animal may experience ongoing pain and discomfort, which can feel like torture. If an animal doesn't get the right food and nutrition over the long term, this can cause serious health problems. If cows have too much corn in their diet, they can get liver

These laying chickens are so crowded, they can't even spread their wings. This causes frustration and stress.
BC SPCA

disease or ulcers. If chickens don't get enough calcium in their food, their bones can get weak and break under their own weight. Overcrowded living conditions, loud noises, uncomfortable heat or cold, angry voices (especially if the angry voices are associated with being hurt) and bullying by people, or even by other animals, can cause animals stress. If a problem doesn't happen very often or is dealt with quickly, the stress and anxiety won't last. But when an animal experiences anxiety, fear, pain or discomfort day after day, this causes distress—especially if animals can't get away from the thing that's hurting or bothering them and feel trapped. They need help before they reach critical distress. Freedom from distress means making sure animals aren't abused and don't live in fear or constant stress.

Large farms where animals are crowded together are one place where ongoing stress will happen if farmers aren't careful. The old-fashioned image of a small family-owned

These beef cattle are packed together on a feedlot (where they're fed mostly grain). JO-ANNE MCARTHUR/ISRAEL AGAINST LIVE SHIPMENTS

farm where chickens get to peck around outside and cows stroll through meadows, munching on grass, is not the reality on most farms today. On large industrial farms (sometimes called factory farms), animals are often kept inside huge windowless barns and never see the outdoors. Chickens can be so crowded together that they can't spread their wings. It used to be common for some farmers to starve their egg-laying hens for periods of 7 to 14 days as a way of getting the hens to lay more eggs. Hunger shocks the chickens' bodies into molting (losing their feathers). After molting, chickens tend to lay more and larger eggs. But the periods of hunger cause ongoing suffering for the chickens. Today Canada and countries in the European Union have regulations that forbid forced molting on farms. The United States is beginning to adopt new regulations as well.

Crowding on industrial farms can lead to stress, injury and the spread of disease. Poor air quality can also cause suffering. JO-ANNE MCARTHUR/ WE ANIMALS

SCIENCE SAYS BE KIND

What do you think these baboons in a zoo are feeling?
PAWEL WEWIORSKI/GETTY IMAGES

One of 66 dogs the BC SPCA rescued from cages at a puppy mill. Their fur was so dirty and matted you couldn't tell their fronts from their backs. BC SPCA

As scientists learn new information about animal biology, behavior and emotions, we gain better insight into how to improve the lives of animals on farms, in zoos and in our homes. People used to think animals didn't have emotions, but research clearly tells us that animals feel happiness, sadness, anger, fear, affection, playfulness, grief and other complex emotions. We're also learning that the body and mind are tied together—for people and for animals. Not only can pain and discomfort cause emotional stress, but emotional stress on its own can lead to physical reactions.

Have you ever noticed how your hands sweat or your stomach feels queasy when you're nervous about something? Animals, too, can start to feel sick or show other physical signs of stress, such as hair loss or rashes. Ongoing stress can lead to behavioral changes and more serious health problems. In zoos, cramped spaces and boredom can

cause animals to pace or overgroom, sometimes pulling out their own feathers or fur (we'll talk more about this in chapter 5). This can happen with pets and farm animals too. On farms, animals crowded into barns can feel constant stress and frustration and are more likely to develop breathing problems and diseases passed from animal to animal. Animals crammed into stuffy trucks and transported long distances are also more prone to panic, injuries and discomfort from heat or cold. The farming industry is only beginning to recognize the suffering that animals endure in transport. You would think it would be in a farmer's interest to reduce these stressful situations, as healthy animals are worth more to the farmer.

THE PROBLEM WITH PUPPY MILLS

"Puppy mills" are places where large numbers of dogs are bred for profit. Conditions are poor. Dogs are often kept in crowded, dirty pens and cages with little attention paid to health or socialization. When animal protection officers

KIDS IN ACTION

KIRA GOLUB

Speaking Out for Animals
Julia Tursi, a high school student from Lansdale, Pennsylvania, has a passion for farm-animal *advocacy*. She's spreading the word about the cruel treatment of animals on factory farms and is also speaking out against puppy mills, calling for a law to end the sale of commercially bred dogs, cats and rabbits in Pennsylvania pet stores. Julia's parents are both veterinarians, so she's been exposed to animal issues since she was very young and felt compelled to help animals from the start. Julia volunteers for the Humane Society of the United States, speaking out about animal issues on social media and raising money to support farm-animal welfare and other projects that help animals.

CARE TIP

BC SPCA

Never Leave a Dog in a Hot Car!
On a hot day a car can quickly become like an oven—even with the windows open. A dog stuck in a hot car will overheat more quickly than a person will. We can sweat, which helps our bodies cool down. Dogs only sweat through their paws. Panting helps them cool down, but it doesn't work well if the air they're breathing is hot. Plus, dogs are covered with warm fur! It takes just 10 minutes for dogs to show symptoms of heat stroke. Signs a dog is in trouble include panting heavily, drooling, appearing drowsy or uncoordinated and having glassy eyes. Dogs will feel anxiety and panic as well. Fifteen minutes in a hot car can put some dogs into critical distress, which means they can collapse into a coma and die.

If you see a dog in a car on a hot day, the dog's guardian is likely in a nearby store. You can ask the store to make an announcement. You can also ask an adult to call the local animal protection agency or police. Stay with the animal and observe. If the guardian does not return to the car quickly, and the dog shows signs of critical distress, call 9-1-1. To treat a dog who has become overheated, remove her from the heat, give her cool water to drink, cool her body down with water and fan vigorously to promote evaporation. This speeds up cooling. Do not put ice on the dog (ice constricts blood vessels and prevents cooling). Call an emergency vet right away.

investigated a puppy mill in Langley, British Columbia, they found overcrowding and neglect. Many of the animals were sick, and the fur of some dogs was so dirty and badly matted, you couldn't tell the front of the animal from the back. Sixty-six dogs were rescued and taken to a shelter for medical attention.

REDUCING STRESS, CREATING HAPPY HOMES

Understanding the characteristics and needs of different animals can help us know which conditions will help an animal thrive in our care. We can change their housing and handling to minimize or eliminate stress. We know that small animals such as gerbils, rats, guinea pigs and rabbits have evolved to fear predators. They feel safer and less stressed if they have a place to hide. If they're kept out in the

Gerbils and other small animals feel less stress if they have places to hide.
CAMILOTORRES/GETTY IMAGES

open or where they can hear predator animals like dogs, cats or hawks nearby, they will feel ongoing distress. The same goes for chickens. If they are in outdoor enclosures that hawks fly over, or that predators like foxes, coyotes or ferrets can access by digging under the walls, they feel fear and stress, because they must always be on alert. Outside enclosures are great for exercise and foraging, but they need to be predator-proof and include safe places that the chickens can duck under to hide. If we think like a chicken, it can help us make sure they are content and healthy.

One of the things animal shelters do to reduce stress is keep cats, dogs and small animals in separate areas. Hearing barking dogs causes stress in cats, just as cats can make prey animals like gerbils and hamsters nervous if they are in the same space. The good thing is that animals aren't in a shelter very long (hopefully). But in a zoo, animals are there for their entire lives.

This backyard chicken coop has both indoor and outdoor space, and it's secure from predators. CHUCKCOLLIER/GETTY IMAGES

Cats at animal shelters feel less stress when they have places to hide and perch and when their food and sleeping area is separate from their litter box. BC SPCA

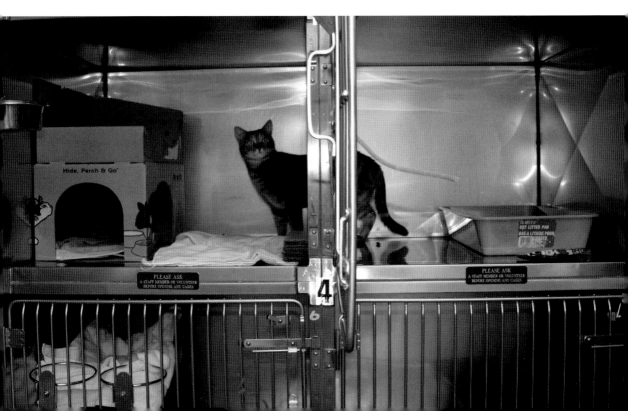

Jacqueline Pearce

Pacing around a small space is boring and stressful for animals in zoos. BC SPCA

It used to be that zoo animals were kept in barren cages, with no place to get away from people. After all, people were paying to see the animals. Welfare concerns were secondary. Zoo animals did not do well and lived short lives. Today the best zoos aim to reduce animal stress by creating enclosures that mimic an animal's natural environment. This means including things animals can use for climbing, hiding, exploring and foraging, and time-out areas where they can escape from other animals and the stares of watching humans. Any confinement, however, whether in a cage or a larger, more natural-looking enclosure, causes ongoing stress to wild animals who evolved in rich ecosystems where they could roam and explore. Exotic animals such as snakes, lizards and parrots also experience extreme stress when they are taken from the wild and kept as pets. They might live, but they seldom thrive in captive environments.

WHERE'S MY MOTHER?

Kittens and puppies may experience fear and anxiety if they are taken away from their mother and siblings when they are too young. New research suggests that kittens should stay with their mothers for at least 8 weeks, while puppies should stay for at least 12 weeks.

Most farm and wild animal babies, too, get upset if they're separated from their mothers. There are a few exceptions, such as reptiles, who leave their eggs to hatch on their own. Mother rabbits feed their young for 25 days but don't stay in the nest or burrow with them, because staying away helps keep predators from finding the babies. With most animals, though, instinct tells mothers to keep their babies close and protect them. Everyone knows not to get between a mother bear and her cubs! And the babies know they need to stay close to be fed and feel safe.

But there's more than just survival instinct at play. Studies have found that there is a strong emotional bond between a mother animal and her babies, just like there is between human parents and their children.

Newborn kittens and puppies need their mother's milk and the warmth and security of being together.
BOZHDB/GETTY IMAGES

For most young animals, like these bear cubs, time spent with Mom and siblings is important for learning social and survival skills. There is also an emotional bond.
KENCANNING/GETTY IMAGES

Jacqueline Pearce

THE SOCIAL LIFE OF COWS

Cows are gentle, friendly animals who prefer to live in social groups called herds. Like you and your friends, cattle form close bonds with some members of their group. When left alone, a cow will call out to other cows for connection.

Cows also have a close bond with their calves. When beef cows have babies, the calves stay with their mothers and nurse for several months, then go on to graze with the rest of the herd. Dairy calves, however, are removed from their mothers, usually within 24 hours of birth. Giving birth to a calf gets the mother cow's body producing milk. Once the calf is taken away, the cow can then be milked for human use. Today's cows are bred to produce huge amounts of milk—much more than a single calf would ever drink. The longer a mother and her calf stay together, the stronger the bond between them and the more stressful their separation. Also, mother cows never forget their calves. It is common to see them licking their grown calves just as they did when the

Calves raised for veal are separated from their mothers and placed in small stalls. On this large modern farm, calves have room to turn around, but not much more. On some farms, veal calves have even less room.
CONSTANTINOPRIS/GETTY IMAGES

calves were young. Scientific studies show that calves who are allowed to have contact with their mothers or other cows grow up to be more social adults who get along better with other cows. Cows in a comfortable social group are happier and more at ease. It's also easier for farmers to herd them. Cows living in a social group will all follow the leader into a barn or wherever the farmer needs them to go.

Although dairy calves are taken away from their mothers on modern farms, most female calves are kept on the farm to replace older milk cows. The remaining females and the males are sold for meat. They might be slaughtered at a young age for veal (meat from young calves), or they might be raised along with adult beef cattle for beef. Most veal calves are kept in small individual pens or crates that are about as wide as a school desk. At some veal farms, calves are chained to their pens. They can lie down and get up, but they

Cows like company, and there is a strong bond between mother and calf.
BACKYARD-PHOTOGRAPHY/GETTY IMAGES

Horses, like other animals, give clues to their emotions through body language, heart rate and hormone level.
TABITHA ROTH/GETTY IMAGES

can't play, explore or even turn around. Farmers confine the calves to make feeding and cleaning easier and so the calves' muscles stay weak, which makes the meat more tender.

Living in a small crate and not being able to move properly is both boring and stressful for a calf. Animal welfare organizations are trying to change regulations so that farmers are required to let calves stay longer with their mothers, then live in group housing rather than individual crates. Dairy farms in some parts of the world (such as Canada) are now moving to group housing for calves.

THE SCIENCE BEHIND STRESS

Some animals respond to stressful situations with an increased heart rate. They will also produce the stress hormone called *cortisol*. Both reactions can be recorded and measured, which helps scientists understand which situations produce more or less stress for animals. Cows produce higher levels of cortisol when separated from their herd. Lab rats and mice produce higher levels of cortisol when they're overcrowded. Even fish have elevated cortisol levels when they're overcrowded. So do people.

READING A DOG'S STRESS

Dogs "speak" to people and other dogs through body language. They express their emotions using their eyes, mouths, ears, fur on their backs (hackles), tails and body positions, as well as a number of different barks and growls. For example, a dog with an anxious personality will give clear signals he is uncomfortable when a more confident dog approaches him. The first signals are subtle. He will lick his lips, yawn, blink his eyes and avoid eye contact. If he's feeling increasingly anxious, he will turn his body to the side or even face the opposite direction. He is signaling that he is not a threat and wants to be left alone.

If the threat persists, anxiety turns to fear, and his body language reflects this. The fearful dog will lower his body and tense his muscles. He'll pull back his ears and tuck his tail under his body. He will pant to get more oxygen to his muscles, preparing to either fight or flee. If there is a confrontation, the fearful dog will growl, show teeth and lunge. Once the threat is gone, the dog will begin to relax his muscles by doing a body shake.

Understanding that animals feel both physical and emotional stress, and learning what situations cause stress, can help us make sure animals have freedom from distress.

TRUE OR FALSE?

Animals can smell fear.
True. When many animals (including people) are stressed or frightened, they produce a fear pheromone (pronounced FARE-O-moan). A pheromone is a chemical "scent" that animals can smell. Prey animals (cows, deer and rabbits) will get nervous when they smell other animals' fear pheromones. They will avoid a place that has fear pheromones in the air.

The pheromone is like a silent alarm that lets animals know there could be a danger nearby. Fish, too, release a chemical "alarm" when they are caught or injured. It cues other fish to freeze, dash or hide. When a predator animal (like a lion or wolf) smells a prey animal's fear pheromones, it can trigger the predator's instinct to hunt and chase.

Four
NO PLACE LIKE HOME

We all like to sleep in a comfortable bed, have a warm, cozy home in winter and a cool, shady place to escape from the sun in summer. Animals like to be comfortable too.

My cat's favorite spot to nap is my dog's large cushy bed. Farm and zoo animals aren't so lucky. Some animals kept in barns or zoos are forced to sleep on hard concrete. Others, like egg-laying hens living in small cages (called battery cages), spend all their time standing or resting on wire mesh flooring. The inside of barns might also be crowded, smelly or drafty, depending on the time of year, and full of dust and feces. Farm animals who live outside often don't have a good place to shelter from cold wind and rain or hot sun. They may suffer from discomfort most of their lives.

In Canada, the national Codes of Practice for the Care and Handling of Farm Animals give farmers guidelines for providing their animals with minimum levels of comfort, including protecting animals from changes in weather and temperature. Freedom from discomfort means making sure animals in your care have a safe, comfortable place to live.

Some pets, like my cat Curious and dog, Dylan, enjoy curling up together. J. PEARCE

SOME LIKE IT HOT, SOME LIKE IT COLD

Chihuahuas were bred in the hot climate of Mexico. They typically have very short fur, which helps keep them cool in hot weather. They are accustomed to hot sunny days, and they don't like cold, rain and snow. They prefer to stay indoors on cold days and may need the warmth of a coat if they go outside. Keep in mind that a coat, or other clothing, can hide a dog's hackles or tail, making it harder for other dogs to read her body language.

Dogs with longer fur, large dogs who need lots of exercise and dogs with short, flat snouts, who can't breathe or pant easily, do not do well in heat. But even dogs who like warm weather can become dehydrated and get heat stroke if they stay out in the sun too long. They need a shady place they can retreat to and some cool drinking water.

Dogs such as huskies, who were bred to live in a northern climate, have thick fur and like to run outside and get lots of exercise—even in the snow. These dogs were bred to pull

WHAT FREEDOMS MIGHT THESE CAPTIVE PENGUINS BE MISSING IN A ZOO?

sleds, and they were traditionally kept outside. However, in northern climates even dogs accustomed to living outside in the cold need insulated dog houses that are raised off the frozen ground and have door flaps to keep out drafts.

Many animals you see in zoos, such as lions, giraffes and elephants, originally came from warmer and dryer parts of the world. Zoos in cold geographic areas often keep these animals indoors in the winter. This prevents them from getting cold, but it means they are cooped up in a small space—often with a hard cement floor and not much to look at or do for months at a time. Besides being uncomfortable, they can't get much exercise, and they are bored. Similarly, animals from cold climates, such as polar bears and wolves, don't do well in zoos in hot countries.

Aquarium fish, too, need to live in water that is the right temperature for them. Tropical fish, like clown fish and bettas, need warmer water. Even one degree's difference can mean their home is no longer comfortable and healthy for them.

The best place for tropical fish is in their natural habitats. Clown fish enjoy the warm waters around coral reefs, where they eat and shelter among anemones.
FOTOTRAV/GETTY IMAGES

Making Houses for Northern Dogs
High school and elementary school students in Northern BC worked together to make all-weather dog houses for outside spaces at animal shelters. Teenagers in an industrial arts class at Lakes District Secondary School built the houses, and kids at Babine Elementary School decorated the houses with colorful designs. The younger kids also made blankets from recycled denim to give dogs a warm place to sleep during the area's cold winters.

LAKES ANIMAL FRIENDSHIP SOCIETY

COMFORT ON THE FARM

Temperature is also important for animals who live in barns. It needs to be constant all year. Not too cold in winter and not too hot in summer. To manage temperature, barns need heat in the winter and good ventilation (air movement) all year. But farmers have to watch out for cold drafts or too much dust in the air. By law, they must have backup generators in case the power goes out, or animals will soon suffer.

Farm animals kept outside, like horses, sheep and beef cattle, need places to get out of the sun in summer and out of the wind, rain and snow in winter. They also need a dry place to lie down—for comfort and to keep them healthy. Damp ground can lead to an infection called foot rot in horses, cows, goats and sheep, which causes pain and lameness. Wet, urine-soaked bedding and damp walls also encourage mold to grow, which can cause breathing and other health problems for animals and farmers.

Pets kept in our homes also need comfortable, dry, clean places to hang out and sleep. This means cleaning litter boxes regularly (to keep the smell down) and keeping hay,

Goats, horses and other farm animals need clean, dry hay for bedding.
ANDYWORKS/GETTY IMAGES

bedding and digging materials fresh in gerbil, hamster and other small-animal enclosures. Remember, if it stinks to you, it really stinks to animals, since most animals have a better sense of smell than we do.

PULLING IN THE RIGHT DIRECTION

If you carry a backpack to school, you might notice that wide, flat, padded straps are more comfortable than skinny straps. It's the same for dogs and their collars and harnesses. It's important for a dog to have a collar, because the dog's ID tag, license and leash get attached to it. But the type of collar makes a big difference. Choke, prong and shock collars use pain to stop a dog from pulling. A choke collar is a chain that tightens when the dog tries to run or pull ahead, forcing him to stop. Choke collars can cause bruising and whiplash and even cut off oxygen. Prong and shock collars work similarly. When the dog pulls, prongs pinch the skin around his neck. With a shock collar, when the dog pulls, the collar gives the animal an electrical shock. A shock collar is not only painful

CARE TIP

Wheely Comfy
A wheel is a good way for a hamster to get exercise. It's important to choose one that's safe and comfortable. Solid surfaces are better than wire ones (the wire can hurt the hamster's feet). The wheel should be large enough that a hamster's back isn't forced to bend into a U shape when he runs. Other small animals, such as mice, gerbils and rats, can use wheels too. The same guidelines for comfort apply—find a wheel that won't cramp their backs or catch their feet or tails as they run.

KRBLOKHIN/GETTY IMAGES

Dogs need comfortable collars for attaching IDs and leashes. A good-fitting padded harness can also make walking your dog easier. SOLSTOCK/GETTY IMAGES

but also causes ongoing fear and anxiety (distress). These collars are considered cruel by animal welfare groups.

Flat collars that buckle or clip together are comfortable options—as long as they are the right fit for the size and weight of your dog. For dogs who tend to pull, a properly fitted head halter is a way to curb the dog's pulling without causing pain. Harnesses can provide more comfort and security for some dogs—especially small dogs or dogs who have eye or breathing issues that are made worse by pressure on the neck from a collar. Ideally a good-fitting, comfortable collar or harness should be accompanied by training. Positive reinforcement, which gives dogs rewards for following directions, is a recommended method of training.

AGING ANIMALS' CHANGING NEEDS

If you have an older dog, maybe you've noticed that it's not as easy as it used to be for her to climb stairs or jump in and out of a car. Cats and other animals will also slow down and not be able to climb or move as easily as they once did. An older dog might need a ramp to get out of your car and a softer bed for aching bones and joints. Cats who used to have their food dishes or sleeping spots up high might need food,

As animals get older they slow down, and they need different food and more frequent vet visits. CATHERINE FALLS COMMERCIAL/GETTY IMAGES

water and sleeping spots closer to the ground. They may have different food needs as well and will need to see a vet more often. These actions provide freedom from discomfort.

A group of stray cats living together outside is called a cat colony. Abandoned or homeless cats and dogs (and sometimes rabbits) are vulnerable to harsh weather, hunger and disease.
SHAUNL/GETTY IMAGES

HOMES FOR EVERYONE

Put a male and female cat together, or a male and female dog, and you could end up with kittens or puppies you don't have room for and can't afford to take care of. Many cities around the world have a problem with pet overpopulation, which means homeless cats or dogs are wandering the streets, often starving and unhealthy. Giving them operations that prevent them from having babies—which is called spaying with females and neutering with males—helps reduce the number of homeless animals and makes it easier to ensure that there is a good home for every dog and cat.

DID YOU KNOW?

Whales Can Get Sunburned

In the wild, whales and dolphins can swim deep in the ocean, far from the reach of the sun's rays. In captivity, orcas and dolphins often get sunburned because the pools they are kept in are too shallow for them to escape from the sun. Some aquariums even paint orcas with black zinc oxide to prevent and conceal sunburn.

HABITATS UNDER THREAT

The Five Freedoms are usually applied to animals in our direct care—pets, farm and zoo animals (and sometimes injured wildlife). Wild animals take care of themselves and do best when we leave them alone. But what happens when our actions threaten wildlife and their homes?

Human activities such as **deforestation**, **urbanization** and pollution are disrupting the natural habitats of wild animals all around the world. Burning **fossil fuels** (coal, oil and gas) and cutting down the world's forests (deforestation) also contribute to climate change. The rise in global temperature is a particularly big problem for animals in colder climates. Polar bears live and travel on sea ice, hunting seals, walruses and birds—animals who also depend on sea ice. As the ice disappears, so does the polar bears' food source. The hungry bears are forced to come onto dry land and look for food where people live—often garbage dumps and backyards.

When we think about the world as an animal home affected by our actions, environmental concerns and the Five Freedoms overlap.

Human activities are causing climate change, which means polar bears and other Arctic animals are losing the sea ice they call home.
STAN TEKIELA AUTHOR / NATURALIST / WILDLIFE PHOTOGRAPHER/GETTY IMAGES

Five
DOING WHAT COMES NATURALLY

Do you have a favorite thing you like to do—something that makes you feel happy? Maybe it's playing soccer, drawing pictures, climbing trees or just hanging out with family or friends. There are things animals like to do that make them feel happy and content as well. Chickens like to scratch for food and stretch their wings. Cows like to graze on grass alongside other cows and sometimes rub against a tree to scratch an itch. Dogs like to go for walks, play and hang out with their pack (whether it's a dog pack or their human family). Gerbils like to dig underground tunnels and dens and gnaw on things. Lizards like to explore and bask in the sun. Parrots like to fly with their flocks.

All animals have their own natural behaviors. If they don't get to do these things, they becomes frustrated and unhappy. Freedom to express behaviors that promote well-being means providing opportunities for animals to do the normal things that make them happy and allow them to thrive in your care. It means letting them be themselves!

People and other animals all have things they like to do that make them happy.
SKYNESHER/GETTY IMAGES

Many animal welfare scientists suggest this is the freedom most overlooked, especially in farming and zookeeping.

HOW DO WE KNOW WHAT ANIMALS WANT TO DO?

Some dogs like to fetch. Some don't. Some cats like to drink water from a dish. Some like to drink from a tap. Chances are, you know what kinds of things your pets prefer, even though they've never told you. You were able to figure it out by giving them choices and watching what they do.

Of course, farm animals have likes and dislikes too. Scientists have come up with tests to measure these things. Called preference tests, they "ask" animals what they want (or prefer) and how badly they want it. In these experiments, animals are usually given a choice between different food, bedding or things to do. The tests ask questions like, Do you want to stay in a cage or go outside? Would you rather sleep on concrete, a rubber mat or sand? Which food do you like better? Would you like to live alone or in a group? The option animals pick more often or spend more time with is the one they prefer.

These hens in battery cages have no room to nest, forage, dust bathe, perch or spread their wings—all things chickens love to do. They also have to stand on a wire floor.
BARBARAGIBBBONS/GETTY IMAGES

BATH TIME FOR CHICKENS

Have you ever seen a bird sit in sandy soil and flap her wings like she's taking a bath with no water? Dust bathing is a natural behavior for egg-laying hens and other birds. It helps remove parasites and keeps their feathers clean and healthy. Given the chance, hens will spend up to half an hour a day dust bathing.

In an experiment, scientists gave egg-laying hens a choice of different materials for dust bathing. The hens dust bathed more often and for longer in sand and peat (which are composed of smaller, finer particles) than in straw or wood shavings. On large modern farms, most egg-laying hens spend their entire lives in small wire cages (battery cages). They can't dust bathe at all. It's such an important behavior, though, that the hens still pretend to dust bathe on the wire floor. They scratch, rub and shake like they would during a real dust bath. On *free run* farms, hens live in a large open house called an aviary, and they can dust bathe on the floor. On *free range* farms, chickens can also go outside and dust bathe there.

HOW BADLY DO THEY WANT IT?

Some preference tests get animals to "work" for what they want by pulling a lever, pressing a button or pushing a door. Scientists slowly make the task harder. They ask questions like How many times will an animal pull the lever for food? How heavy does the door have to be before an animal stops pushing it to go outside? The more work animals are willing to do, the more their preferred option means to them. Remember those cows in chapter 1, who used the nose pump to get fresh water—even in the summer when they had easier-to-get water available?

PASTURE, PLEASE!

Cows are grazing animals by nature. They like to walk around and munch on grass. Grazing fields are called pastures. In the past it was common for all cows to go outside to graze, but on modern farms in North America, most dairy cows are raised in barns and fed hay and silage (a mix of grasses and plants) plus grain. How important is pasture to dairy cows? Scientists designed an experiment to find out.

KIDS IN ACTION

CARRIE PLUMMER

A Happy Place for Farm Animals
Henry Plummer is a young animal advocate from the Upper Peninsula of Michigan. He's a vegan and is committed to helping wildlife and farm animals. Henry encourages his friends and community to help animals and raise money for animal welfare organizations such as SASHA Farm, a sanctuary and safe haven for farm animals in Manchester, MI. SASHA Farm provides food, shelter, vet care and companionship to more than 200 animals. Many were neglected, mistreated and in danger of dying before finding a safe, permanent home at SASHA Farm. In 2018, when Henry was 10 years old, he was awarded the first Detroit Zoological Society Humane Youth Award.

The cows were trained to push a heavy gate, which weighed more than 132 pounds (60 kilograms). In the first part of the experiment, cows pushed the gate to get to fresh food (a mix of corn and grass silage, hay and mash) in the barn. In the second part of the experiment, the cows had free access to the fresh food, and the weight was added to a gate leading outside to pasture.

Cows worked at least as hard to access pasture as they did to access the fresh feed, and they worked hardest to get outside in the evening hours. This suggests that the cows were interested in going outside not just to eat—especially on summer evenings when it was pleasantly cool outside for walking and grazing.

Despite what preference tests show, most large-scale dairy farms don't want to change, because in North America it's too expensive to buy land to use for grazing. Organic farms, however, are required to provide cows with access to pasture, and these farmers notice that their cows are more content, more physically fit and have fewer hoof and leg injuries.

Grazing outdoors means these cows get to eat grass, exercise, socialize and breathe in the fresh air! BC SPCA

This mother pig and her piglets look happy in their warm, soft nest. Compare them to the pigs in the metal farrowing crate on page 24. BC SPCA

THE NEED TO NEST

Before they give birth, wild sows (female pigs) build nests out of vegetation, such as twigs, bark, grass and leaves. Sows on farms want to nest-build too. But they are kept in metal stalls, or crates, with concrete floors and no room or materials for making a nest. Scientists wanted to know how strongly sows are motivated to build nests for their piglets. They designed an experiment in which sows had to press a button to open a door. The door led to a pen where they could gather straw for nesting. Once the sows learned to press the button, researchers waited longer before opening the door. Some sows pressed the button 300 times just to open the door once. They really wanted that straw!

Sows who live in metal stalls still want to build nests, and they go through the motions of nest building. They root and paw at the bare concrete floor like they're trying to make a real nest. Some progressive farms keep their sows in groups and provide nesting areas for sows and their piglets, but most large industrial farms do not want to incur the cost of changing their barns.

WHAT FISH LIKE

Fish feel safe when they have shadowy places to hide, like they would in the nooks and crannies of a coral reef. In a preference test, a bright light was placed over one section of a fish tank, and then food was added to the tank. Most of the fish preferred to stay in the shady area of the tank than swim out into the light to get the food. Their desire to feel safe was more important than their desire to eat.

ZOO LIFE

In the wild, animals have a variety of natural behaviors. They can forage for food (sometimes traveling great distances), burrow in the ground, climb a tree, swim in the water, patrol their territory, hang out with their friends or search for a mate. In most zoos, enclosures are too small and simple for animals to be very active. Imagine what it would feel like to never leave your bedroom, to be surrounded by the same walls and objects day in and day out for your entire life. Would you get bored?

Hippopotamuses live in groups along rivers in sub-Saharan Africa, staying cool in water and mud and munching on vegetation. What is life like for this hippo in a zoo? ULET IFANSASTI/GETTY IMAGES

This giraffe in a zoo is obsessively licking her lips, a stress behavior.
RAINERVONBRANDIS/GETTY IMAGES

Like us, when animals don't have enough space or things to do, they become frustrated. They can even develop a mental illness known as **zoochosis** and obsessive behaviors called stereotypies (stare-ee-oh-tip-ees). Stereotypies are abnormal actions that are repeated over and over without a real purpose. Some animals sway to and fro, pace, circle or rock back and forth. Others lick walls, chew fences or even bite themselves. In the wild, lions typically walk more than 6 miles (10 kilometers) a day. Stuck in the small space of a zoo, a lion will often pace back and forth, a sign of extreme frustration and boredom. Many animals in zoos become depressed and give up. They might stare into space and stop eating. The overgrooming behaviors mentioned in chapter 3 are also examples of stereotypies.

Why Turtles Cross the Road

During mating season (spring to fall), box turtles are often seen crossing roads in eastern North America, from Ontario to Florida. Male box turtles move from pond to pond, looking for mates. The female turtles also travel, searching for places to lay their eggs. Box turtles have a brown to tan rounded upper shell, patterned with yellowy spots, blotches or lines—kind of like a camouflaged round box. The first time I saw a box turtle, I thought someone had left an army helmet on the ground.

Hundreds of box turtles are injured or killed by cars every year. If you live in an area where these turtles live, you can mount an education campaign to alert drivers to watch for turtles on the road. If you see a turtle trying to cross, stop and carefully pick the turtle up and move him off the road in the direction he was going. But wear gloves or sanitize your hands immediately afterward, as turtles and other reptiles carry **salmonella**, which can make people very sick. Alternatively, place a car mat or cardboard under the turtle, then carefully slide the turtle off the road.

Some zoos are worse than others. The same goes for circuses. Animals are kept in cramped cages and sometimes have poor diets. The only exercise most circus animals get is when they are performing. Small roadside zoos and animal displays often have particularly poor animal welfare standards, partly because they can be run by people with no training in animal care, and there is no one to check up on them. They also may not have much money to enrich the habitats.

A few zoos, such as the Detroit Zoo in Michigan, have made changes to improve the lives of the animals who live there. They give animals larger enclosures to explore and roam around in. They also provide "enrichment," which means more things for animals to do. They plant trees and bushes, add rocks, ropes and logs, and give animals toys to play with. They also scatter or hide food for animals to find, and they provide places for animals to retreat to when they are tired of being watched by human visitors. But it is

What Freedoms are missing for this tiger in a barren zoo in Cambodia? Small roadside zoos and backyard enclosures (which are illegal in many places) can be even worse.
JO-ANNE MCARTHUR/WE ANIMALS

difficult for zoos to provide enough space and opportunities for natural behavior to keep animals such as bears, cougars, wolves, giraffes, elephants, birds or even frogs and reptiles happy and healthy in captivity. In fact, at most zoos the nice vegetation and places to explore are actually for you to see. Look carefully. Often the lush trees and fresh vegetation are surrounded by electric fences to protect them from the animals and keep them looking nice for human visitors.

WHALES AND DOLPHINS

Have you ever seen a whale leap out of the water and crash back down with a huge splash? This behavior is called breaching, and it's pretty impressive even if you only see it on a nature show. Scientists believe that when whales breach or slap the water with a tail or fin, they are sending a message to other whales. Whales also communicate through groans, grunts, clicks and whistles that can travel across hundreds of miles of ocean.

Orcas are social animals who communicate with each other through leaps, splashes and vocal sounds. SHARRON PALMER-HUNT

Scientific research has shown that whales and other cetaceans (marine mammals like dolphins and porpoises) not only communicate but also have social lives, strong

Orcas naturally swim long distances every day. For a whale, living in an aquarium is like a person being stuck alone in a tiny closet for their whole life. JO-ANNE MCARTHUR/WE ANIMALS

bonds with other whales and highly developed memories and problem-solving skills. In their ocean homes, they regularly dive to depths of 328 feet (100 meters), can go as deep as 850 feet (260 meters) and can swim up to 100 miles (160 kilometers) in a day. People didn't know much about whales when the first orca was captured and placed in an aquarium in the early 1960s (she died after injuring herself trying to escape her enclosure). We now know that whales are complex creatures whose Five Freedoms cannot be met in captivity.

Public pressure has persuaded some aquariums, such as the Vancouver Aquarium in Canada, to stop keeping whales and dolphins in captivity. The country also has a new law that makes it illegal to buy or sell cetaceans. But the estimated 51 beluga whales, 5 bottlenose dolphins and 40-year-old orca already living at Marineland in Ontario will likely live the remainder of their lives in captivity. However, whale researchers hope to build a huge ocean pen off the coast of North America where the captive whales can live out the rest of their lives and have their Five Freedoms met.

Cats in the wild stalk and pounce on prey. Batting at a moving toy helps your cat get exercise and use her hunting instinct in a playful way. BC SPCA

KEEPING PETS HAPPY

Making sure your dog, cat, hamster or other pet gets the right food, water, shelter, exercise and vet care is a great start. But like other animals, pets need the fifth freedom—the freedom to express natural behaviors. Otherwise they will suffer frustration and boredom and even get depressed.

Cats need a scratching post, places they can leap to and boxes to hide in. Dogs need to sniff and explore new places outside. We often see photos of snakes coiled up, but snakes have long bodies, and they like to stretch out to their full length. Unfortunately most snakes kept as pets or in zoos or research labs are not given enough space to extend their bodies properly or move around. Like people, snakes need enough room to change their body positions, extend to their natural length and get some exercise.

All animals need variety and stimulation in their lives. You can place food inside a special plastic ball that guinea

CARE TIP

Help Cats Climb the Walls

While dogs are content to live with us at ground level, cats love to climb, balance on ledges and sit up high where they can watch the action from above. Your cat's wild ancestors were jungle cats who perched in trees and climbed rocky ledges where they could overlook the forest floor, watching for prey. Trees and cliffs were also safe places to hang out, groom and sleep.

Today's house cats still behave like wild cats. Yet we often don't provide them with opportunities to climb and perch. Knowing what cats like means you can look at your house from your cat's perspective. Often there are easy ways to create vertical spaces for your cat. Adding step shelves allows your cat to climb the walls. Tall scratching posts with places to hide and perch are also great options for cats. For cats who aren't content to stay indoors, you can create an enclosed "catio" to provide a safe and interesting outdoor space for your cat.

pigs and rabbits roll to get at. It gives them a challenge and gets their bodies moving. Hide a special treat and ask your dog to find it. Let her follow her nose! You can also create exercise pens for guinea pigs, rats and other small animals that provide space for them to explore, safe nesting materials and objects for them to crawl over, hide behind or chew. Watch what they like to do and experiment with new items while they're in their exercise pens. This is how you can give your pets their fifth freedom—the freedom to express behaviors that promote well-being. They'll show their happiness!

Six

BUILDING CARING COMMUNITIES

WE'RE ALL IN THIS TOGETHER

There are many ways people around the world work to ensure that animals in their care have the Five Freedoms. Vets, workers at animal shelters and animal protection officers help animals as part of their jobs. Others volunteer for animal welfare organizations, rescue groups or animal refuges. Some people work to improve laws and regulations to make life better for farm or zoo animals. Others work to help save endangered wildlife or help rehabilitate injured wildlife. Some people simply enjoy having pets as part of their family and providing them with a good life. Even a small act of kindness, such as carefully removing a bee or bug from your house and placing it outside rather than squishing it, makes a difference.

Vet technician Nicole McClelland helps animals in many ways, including feeding this calf. BC SPCA

CARING FOR SICK AND INJURED ANIMALS

Nicole McClelland knew she wanted to work with animals ever since she was a young girl, inspired by her first dog, George. As a trained veterinary technician (someone who

KIDS IN ACTION

EKATERINA BOLSHAKOVA

How a Talent for Art Helps Animals in Need

When Pavel Abramov from Arzamas, Russia, was eight years old, he wanted to do something to help animals in memory of his beloved cat, Barsik. What can a small volunteer do? With help from others, Pavel organized charity events to raise awareness about homeless animals and raise money for his local dog shelter. Pavel, who is a budding artist, also painted pet portraits in exchange for food and other supplies needed by the shelter. Pavel and his Kind Paintbrush project have helped feed over 100 dogs at the Arzamas shelter.

helps vets), she's assisted with surgery on a mouse, cared for diabetic cats, looked after dogs hit by cars, helped sick chickens and cows, and treated a baby raccoon who fell out of a tree. She's also traveled around the world as a volunteer, helping with animal health checks and spaying and neutering in low-income and remote areas.

ANIMAL SHELTERS

In many cities around the world, animal shelters are places that take care of homeless animals. These are animals who were lost, abandoned, rescued from cruel situations or brought in by people who could no longer take care of their pet. Shelters are usually operated by nonprofit organizations and funded through their city or donations from people in the community. Shelter workers and volunteers take care of the animals until they are adopted by someone. Unfortunately, not all shelter animals find a new home. If you and your family are thinking of getting a pet, an animal shelter is a place where you can find animals in need of a good home.

As a shelter manager and now chief operations officer at the BC SPCA, Parm Takhar assists all kinds of animals, including these rescued husky pups.
BC SPCA

HELPING HOMELESS CATS

Animal shelters deal with thousands of homeless cats each year. Some cats are left at the shelter when their guardians have to move or for some other reason can no longer take care of them. Other cats are rescued from **animal hoarders**, when conditions in the home have become crowded and unhealthy. Some cats may have been lost or abandoned or grown up in feral cat colonies, where domestic cats are living on their own. Many cats left on their own outside die from starvation, disease, injury or attack by predators. Those who survive end up having kittens, which means even more homeless cats.

In cities like Vancouver, British Columbia, animal welfare organizations rescue feral cats. They trap the cats humanely and bring them to clinics for medical exams,

Homeless cats are a community responsibility. ARINA_BOGACHYOVA/ GETTY IMAGES

vaccinations, identification tattoos, spaying and neutering and treatment for any other medical issues. Kittens and tamer adult cats can then be adopted into new homes. Cats who are too wild to live with people are returned to the feral cat colonies, and volunteers bring food and water every day and watch for medical issues.

INVESTIGATING CRUELTY

Unfortunately, not everyone takes good care of their pets or farm animals. Some people don't understand what their animals need, or perhaps they don't have enough money to provide good food, shelter and medical care. Others get sick, or they have family emergencies and their pets are unintentionally neglected. In some cases, people hurt animals on purpose because they are bullies who lack empathy, or they may have mental health issues.

Cruelty investigators rescue a cat trapped in a house during an evacuation from wildfires in BC.
BC SPCA

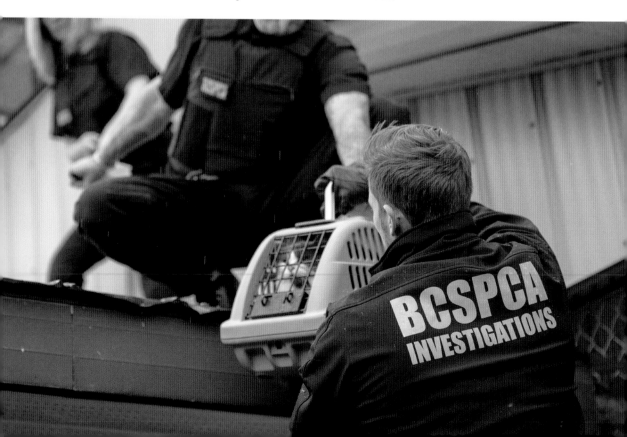

When someone sees animals they think are being mistreated or neglected, they can report it to their local Society for the Prevention of Cruelty to Animals (SPCA) or humane society. These organizations will send animal protection officers to investigate. Animal protection officers think about the Five Freedoms when deciding if they need to intervene in a situation. First, they will check whether all the animal's needs are being met. Then they will ask the animal's guardian to make appropriate changes to improve conditions for the animal.

The investigating officers will give the guardian time to make the changes, then come back to see if the improvements have been made. If problems have not been fixed or animals need immediate medical attention, the officers can get a warrant to take the animals into custody and take them to a shelter or vet. In cases where someone intentionally hurts an animal, or knows they are causing suffering by not providing good care, they can be charged with animal cruelty under the law. Animal protection officers gather evidence to support cruelty charges.

This neglected dog chained in a backyard was reported to animal cruelty investigators and rescued. BC SPCA

EMERGENCY HELP

When fires, floods and other natural disasters strike, animal protection organizations and volunteers help rescue and look after animals until they can be reunited with their human families. After the devastating earthquake and tsunami in Japan in 2011, rescuers dug dogs and cats out of the rubble and put on protective gear to rescue animals left behind when people were forced to evacuate the area surrounding a damaged nuclear reactor.

In 2017, a bad wildfire year, more than 1,000 fires swept across British Columbia. Hundreds of people had to flee their homes, leaving their pets and farm animals behind. The BC SPCA set up animal evacuation centers at several locations, and cruelty investigators went behind the fire lines to rescue animals. As well as cats and dogs, they rescued and sheltered cows, horses, a few birds, fish and even a snake. In 2018, after Hurricane Michael hit Florida, the ASPCA helped the Florida State Animal Response Coalition rescue and care for animals left behind when their guardians had to flee.

During natural disasters and other emergencies, the ASPCA works to rescue animals and reunite them with their guardians. COPYRIGHT © 2020. THE AMERICAN SOCIETY FOR THE PREVENTION OF CRUELTY TO ANIMALS (ASPCA). ALL RIGHTS RESERVED.

The ASPCA assisted Florida State Animal Response Coalition (Florida SARC) to rescue and care for animals impacted by Hurricane Michael in 2018. COPYRIGHT © 2020. THE AMERICAN SOCIETY FOR THE PREVENTION OF CRUELTY TO ANIMALS (ASPCA). ALL RIGHTS RESERVED.

CARE TIP

Preparing Your Pet for a Disaster

Do you have a disaster plan for your family and pets? What would you do if you had to flee a fire or survive an earthquake? Talk with your family about what to do if there is an emergency such as a fire, flood, hurricane or earthquake. Be prepared.

Make an evacuation plan that includes your pets.

- Have a pet first-aid kit.
- Get your pets microchipped and make sure their IDs are up to date.
- Keep travel carriers and leashes in a handy location—and get your pets used to being in their carriers.
- Put together an emergency kit that includes pet food, bottled water, a travel litter box or puppy pee pads, pet toys, medications and vaccination and medical info, as well as a list of local evacuation shelters where people can stay with their pets or contact info for an animal shelter you can take your pets to if you can't keep them with you.
- Place a rescue-alert sticker on the front door of your house to let firefighters and other emergency responders know there are pets inside. Include how many pets and what kind. If you leave with your pets, write *evacuated* on the sticker so emergency responders will know the pets are no longer in the house.

BC SPCA

WILDLIFE REHAB

People who help sick, injured or orphaned wildlife are called rehabilitators (or rehabbers). They take care of the animals, often at wildlife rehabilitation centers, then release them back into the wild. They have to handle wildlife calmly and carefully to keep the animals from becoming too stressed. Rehabbers also need to make sure wild animals don't get used to being around people. They do this by handling them as little as possible, sometimes hiding behind barriers, wearing masks or using an animal puppet to do the feeding.

In the wild, being afraid of people helps keep animals safe and out of harm's way. Many injuries occur when wildlife get too close to people. For example, a deer might get hit by a car, a bear or raccoon could get stuck in garbage, an owl

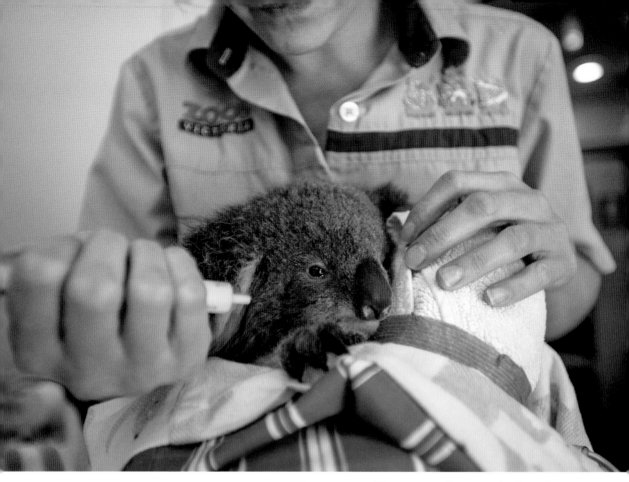

A young koala, who was injured and lost her mother during the 2020 Australian bushfires, receives milk and medical care from Australian RSPCA workers and volunteers.
JO-ANNE MCARTHUR/WE ANIMALS

or coyote could get poisoned by a pesticide, a songbird might be attacked by a pet cat, and an otter or a seabird might be caught in an oil spill. Rehabbers need to make sure the animals have recovered and regained their abilities to take care of themselves before releasing them back into the wild.

HABITAT PROTECTION

Around the world, many animals are dying because their homes and habitats are being destroyed. In Indonesian Borneo thousands of orangutans die each year as the tropical forest where they live is cut down. In place of the natural forest, large corporations plant African palm oil trees to make palm oil, which is used in many household products sold around the world. Palm oil can be found in ice cream, chocolate and other candies, shampoo, soap and household cleaners. Wildlife preservation and conservation groups and scientists are working to stop deforestation and educate people about disappearing habitats and animal species. They're asking people to shop with wildlife in mind, to check ingredients and not buy products that contain palm oil.

STOPPING THE TRADE IN EXOTIC ANIMALS

Habitat loss is the biggest threat to wildlife, but some animals are also endangered because they are caught, sold and often die in the exotic animal trade. Elephants are still killed for their ivory. Alligator, crocodile, snake and kangaroo skin is made into boots, wallets and other accessories. Tigers, rhinos, **pangolins** and various other endangered animals are captured and killed for use in traditional medicines, while many reptiles, amphibians, parrots and tropical fish are

DID YOU KNOW?

The World's Biggest Bat Cave Needed a Hero

Bracken Cave, on the northern outskirts of San Antonio, TX, is home to the world's largest bat colony, with more than 15 million Mexican free-tailed bats. Female bats gather there each year to give birth and rear their young. Mexican free-tailed bats help farmers by eating corn earworm moths and other crop pests. Bats at the Bracken colony are estimated to consume over 100 tons (91 metric tonnes) of moths every summer night.

Bats share the natural area with many other animal species, including birds such as the endangered golden-cheeked warbler. In the past the natural plants and animals, bats included, were threatened by the growth of ranching and commercial development. Then, in 1992, conservation groups worked with the community of San Antonio to purchase Bracken Cave and a small chunk of land around it. Now nearly 1,500 acres (607 hectares) of former ranchland surrounding the cave have been purchased, and the area is being restored and preserved so that the bats and other wildlife will continue to have a home where they can thrive.

captured to be sold as pets. As a result of the pet trade, the Chinese tiger gecko is now extinct in the wild.

Many exotic pets we see in North America, such as African gray parrots, sugar gliders (small possums), lizards, geckos, turtles, snakes and tropical reef fish, are wild animals who were captured and taken from their homes. They are often transported and smuggled in terrible conditions, stuffed into buckets or bags or other tight hiding places where they can suffocate, get sick, attacked by other animals and injured or killed. Even after transportation, their needs for food, healthcare and appropriate living conditions often are not met. Seventy-five percent die in the first year. More funding and wildlife protection officers are needed to stop wildlife traffickers. It's also important for people to stop buying exotic animals and endangered-animal products such as clothing.

In Cambodia, the Wildlife Alliance works with local law enforcement officers to stop wildlife traffickers. They rescued 785 endangered tortoises, turtles and snakes from one smuggler's boat.
BELIZAR73/GETTY IMAGES

ANIMAL ACTIVISM

Animal activists are people who take direct action to save animals or draw public attention to situations in which animals are being hurt. Actions range from writing letters or handing out information flyers to participating in public demonstrations and standing on the street in costumes to get people's attention. Animal *rights* activists feel that all animals have the right to healthy, happy lives. Not only are they concerned for the daily welfare of animals, but they also don't want animals to be killed for human food or clothing.

Animal activists work to raise public awareness about the cruelty involved in animal testing, the fur trade, rodeos, circuses, zoos and other situations that cause stress or physical harm to animals. They also work to change or strengthen laws that protect animals, and they encourage people to eat a meat-free diet and not wear leather or fur. Some animal activists have even gone undercover to find out what is happening on factory farms or in labs where animals are used in testing.

Animal activists in Jakarta, Indonesia, dress as forest tigers and orangutans to get people's attention and call for the protection of Indonesian forests and wildlife. YAMTONO_SARDI/GETTY IMAGES

Seven
YOU CAN MAKE A DIFFERENCE

LET'S GET OUT AND PLAY

Around the world, amazing kids are doing things that make a difference for animals, starting small and close to home or helping local, national and international groups with larger projects. As kids learn about the Five Freedoms, they're inspired to improve the lives of their own pets as well as those of other animals. This means recognizing that individual animals have their own unique needs for food, water, healthcare, comfort, security and opportunities to do the things they like to do. When it comes to pets, most animals and kids like to play, so it's pretty easy to find something you both like to do together, whether it's going for walks, playing hide-and-seek and other games or just hanging out.

WORKING TOGETHER

Kids are also helping animals by forming clubs at their schools where they learn about issues, create posters and host events to help educate other kids and adults about animal welfare and environmental issues. Kids have collected

Dog agility activities are mentally challenging, good exercise and fun for both dogs and their human companions.
BC SPCA

Young activists in Toronto, ON, Zionne Jongsma and Jasmine Polsinelli (at right), hand out leaflets about the cruelty of trapping animals and fur farming, discouraging people from wearing fur.
JO-ANNE MCARTHUR/WE ANIMALS

supplies for animals in need and made blankets for shelter animals. Kids have also come up with all kinds of ways to raise money to help animals at local shelters or donate to animal and environmental groups around the world—everything from selling lemonade, cookies or handmade animal toys to donating birthday money and participating in walkathons. Maybe you've done some of these things too.

SPEAKING OUT AGAINST FUR

Jasmine Polsinelli is a young animal advocate from Oshawa, Ontario, who has participated in public demonstrations against the cruelty of trapping and farming animals for their fur. At age 11, she created an educational video on YouTube called *The Truth About Trapping*, encouraging people not to buy clothing made with real animal fur and calling for companies to use cruelty-free products in their outdoor clothing.

CARE TIP

TEN THINGS YOU CAN DO TO HELP ANIMALS

1. Become an expert on your own pet. Find out all you can about the species, breed and individual likes and needs, and do your best to give your pet a good life. If you don't have a pet, pick an animal to learn about.

2. Set aside time every day to play and interact with your animal companion.

4. Learn about your wild neighbors. Watch for birds, mammals and bugs, listen for bird and other animal calls, and look for footprints, holes in trees and other clues to the presence of wildlife. Remember to stay at a respectful distance and keep pets away from wildlife, nests and burrows.

3. Enhance your pet's habitat. You could build a more interesting enclosure for gerbils, hamsters and other small animals, build an enclosed catio for your feline or add step shelves to your walls.

6. Share what you learn with family, friends and others. Make posters, create a newsletter, blog, give a talk at a school assembly or host an animal-movie day.

5. Join or start an animal, environmental or nature club at your school or in your community. Find out about animal issues in your community and around the world.

8. Talk to your family about going meatless, even just one day a week, and look for meatless options when you eat out with family or friends.

7. Think about animals when you're shopping—look for products that don't harm animals or their habitats. And consider alternatives to plastics (balloons, straws, single-use bags and bottles), which can end up in the oceans and harm marine life.

10. Speak out when you see someone doing something unkind or harmful to animals. If the person is a friend or classmate, let them know their actions are not okay. If you see someone else doing something that causes you concern, or you see a pet, farm animal or wild animal in distress, let your teacher or parent know.

9. Be a good example. Be kind to people and animals—even tiny creatures like bees, spiders and other bugs.

CARING ABOUT THE COMFORT OF COMMUNITY CATS

When teens in Kamloops, British Columbia, learned about the issue of cat overpopulation and feral cats, they worked together to take action. Concentrating on the fourth freedom (freedom from discomfort), the teens made 40 outdoor cat shelters out of storage containers and bedding materials. The shelters were set up throughout the community to provide safe, dry and warm spaces for cats living outdoors.

HELPING FARM ANIMALS

Most kids in North America today don't have a lot of interactions with farm animals other than on the occasional school field trip or visits to petting zoos. In a few cities, people are allowed to have backyard chickens, and kids are involved with feeding them and collecting eggs. Some kids, like Henry Plummer in chapter 5, volunteer at farm-animal shelters and sanctuaries, feeding animals, cleaning pens and doing other tasks. Other kids are learning about farm animals and their welfare at school, in animal clubs or even on their own through books and the internet. Some kids are speaking out for more humane farming practices and making food choices that support humane farms.

Kids in the community of Sarhento Mariano cemetery in Pasay City in the Philippines bring street dogs for free vaccinations by Pasay Pups animal welfare charity.
PASAY PUPS

KIDS IN ACTION

A.J. DHALLA

For the Birds

Adam Dhalla is a young photographer and birder from the West Coast of Canada. He can't imagine a world without birds and birdsong, and that's why he's doing everything he can to raise public awareness about worldwide threats to birds. He shares his love of birds with other young people (and adults as well), speaking out about the impacts of habitat loss, pesticides, plastic waste and climate change. He's also developing a mobile game called Find the Birds, which will help kids learn about birds and conservation issues. In 2018, when Adam was 12 years old, he received the Young Birder of the Year Award from the American Birding Association.

REMEMBERING WILD NEIGHBORS

Helping wild animals can be as simple as keeping cats indoors so they don't attack songbirds, sticking decals on your windows to keep birds from flying into them, planting garden flowers and bushes that feed butterflies and bees, wildlife-proofing your garbage cans and respecting all the creatures who share our cities and countryside.

When my daughter was in elementary school, the students painted wall and fence murals to show their vision of a healthy neighborhood, including people, trees and animals. Parents, teachers and students also got together to plant native trees and bushes on the schoolground. The younger students raised salmon fry, then released them into a local stream. In other schools, too, students are learning about local wildlife issues and working together on projects that help wildlife in their communities.

With help from the Stream of Dreams Mural Society, elementary school students in BC create fence murals of swimming fish to help raise awareness about nearby streams. J. PEARCE

CONCLUSION

As our lives have changed over the past few hundred years, so have our relationships with animals. We no longer look at animals as magical creatures or as objects for people to use, as some societies did in the past. Today we understand that animals are unique beings with their own needs, that most have the capacity to feel happiness, affection, sadness and pain, and the ability to think and make choices.

We also know that people, animals and nature are connected. We all rely on clean air and water. When a river or lake is polluted, it affects insects, fish, animals and people. When a forest burns on one side of the world, local animals and people lose their homes, and there is an impact on the rest of the world through changes in air quality and an increase in the greenhouse gases that influence global climate change.

Some countries do better at taking care of animals than others. In places where many people live in poverty, life is also harder for animals. In general, the European Union has higher standards and stricter requirements for how animals

Animals can be good helpers and companions. They make our lives better, and it's our responsibility to make sure their lives are good as well.
LISEGAGNE/GETTY IMAGES

When you're thinking about animals in any situation, such as this rodeo, remember that animals feel hunger, discomfort and pain, as well as fear, frustration and other emotions. BC SPCA

are treated, especially in farming. Many countries do well at some things, but not others. In India cows are considered sacred and people treat them very well—but India also has a high number of homeless animals and a record of treating elephants poorly. At the time of this writing, Canada is doing better than the United States at farm practices in that Canada has national codes that set minimum welfare standards. The United States does not—laws and recommended practices tend to differ from state to state. However, Canada's codes are not enforced, and the farming industry regulates itself. In the United States, California has higher standards than other states. Canada's rating for animal treatment also drops because it continues to allow harp seals, hooded seals and gray seals to be killed for their fur. However, commercial hunting of whitecoats—harp seal pups—is now illegal.

Positive changes can happen through education, laws and regulations (and their monitoring and enforcement), and programs that help animals in need. The actions of individuals can make a huge difference too.

KIND THOUGHTS TO KIND ACTIONS

There are many things that make life good—family, friends, food, books, movies, video games, sports, health, clean air, trees and birds. Your list might be different from mine and different from your best friend's. But we can work together to make sure life is good for everyone in our community—people *and* animals. The Five Freedoms can help us make thoughtful and compassionate choices when it comes to animals.

THINKING ABOUT ANIMALS WITH HELP FROM THE FIVE FREEDOMS

Is your family thinking about getting a pet and how to meet that pet's needs? Wondering how those puppies, kittens or fish in a pet store are doing? Have you noticed pet cats or rabbits living on their own outside? Thought about the lions or elephants in a zoo? Or the horses and bulls at a rodeo? What about the wild animals who live in your city? Or the animals who live in a threatened rainforest on the other side of the world? You can use the Five Freedoms as a tool to help you think about how our actions affect animals and help you decide if animals in a situation are doing okay or need some help.

DID YOU KNOW?

Schools Lend a Chimney

Vaux's swifts are birds who used to roost in hollow old-growth snags in parts of western North America, but with old-growth forests disappearing, the birds often roost in old chimneys. On their migration in early fall each year, the birds stop to roost in the chimneys of two schools in Oregon, Chapman Elementary School in Portland and Hedrick Middle School in Medford. Kids, teachers and parents rallied to protect the birds, ensuring that school furnaces stayed off until the swifts had left. When new furnaces that don't need chimneys were installed, the schools saved and upgraded their chimneys for the swifts' use. The school communities also hold events to celebrate and educate people about the returning birds.

Remember to look for signals for how your pet is feeling. How does your dog, cat or other pet let you know what they like or don't like? HALFPOINT/GETTY IMAGES

the FIVE FREEDOMS

1. Freedom from hunger and thirst

2. Freedom from pain, injury and disease

3. Freedom from distress

4. Freedom from discomfort

5. Freedom to express behaviors that promote well-being

An easy way to give your guinea pigs or rabbit the fifth freedom is to let them have outside playtime in a safe enclosure while you keep watch.
BC SPCA

As you consider each freedom, think about the needs and preferences of the animal in question. Think about the current situation. How are the animal's needs being met? Are some needs not being met or not being met as well as they could be? The answers to these questions can help you decide whether an animal is having a good life or if changes need to be made. If you're thinking about getting a pet, the Five Freedoms can help your family decide if a certain kind of animal is the right pet for you. You might not get a snake or a lizard because it is very difficult and expensive to meet their Five Freedoms. Do you have space, time and energy for a young dog who needs training and lots of exercise? Or do you have a quieter home and lifestyle that might suit an older dog, a cat or a guinea pig? Where do you think is the best place to find your pet? Is it a pet store, a breeder or an animal shelter? Don't forget the costs. Can you afford to make sure your pet has good food, other supplies and vet care?

You can also consider the Five Freedoms to help you make decisions about buying animal products. For example, should you buy clothing made with animal fur or skin, or is there a better choice? Should you buy the eggs from hens who live on a crowded factory farm or hens who live on a free range farm with access to places to perch, dust bathe and forage? Should you visit a zoo, or an aquarium that has captive whales or dolphins? If you go, think about the Five Freedoms and the animals' points of view. To what degree do their circumstances and treatment allow them the Five Freedoms?

Sometimes decisions are not easy to make, but asking questions and thinking things over is a good place to start. If you see an animal in trouble, act. Tell your friends about the Five Freedoms. And if you want to make changes in your own life that are positive for animals, don't forget that it's okay to start small. You can still make a difference.

At the end of the day, the things that make the animals in our lives happy are often the same things that make us happy.

For animals and for us, a good life begins at home. KATE_SEPT2004/GETTY IMAGES

GLOSSARY

advocacy—activity by an individual or group that publicly supports, defends or pleads on behalf of others, such as people or animals who need help, or argues for a particular action or law

anesthetics—drugs that induce temporary insensitivity to pain before a medical procedure.

animal hoarder—a person who takes in a large number of cats, dogs, reptiles or other animals and is unable to give them proper care. Animal hoarding is a compulsive behavior that the person may be unable to stop, and it was recently recognized as a mental health disease.

animal welfare—the well-being of nonhuman animals. Animal welfare is also a branch of science that studies animals' abilities to cope with their environments in situations where people interact with animals—agriculture, entertainment, companionship, research, etc. This research is incorporated into animal welfare standards. The Five Freedoms are all aspects of animal welfare.

antibiotics—drugs used to fight bacterial infections

branding—burning a permanent mark on an animal to identify the animal's owner, commonly done to cattle, horses and sheep kept on open ranges

castrating—removing or inactivating the testicles of a male, which prevents the animal from reproducing and reduces the hormones that cause males to be aggressive. Also known as neutering.

certified humane—designation that tells consumers animal products such as beef, chicken meat, pork, dairy and eggs are from farms with higher welfare standards than on conventional farms. The certification is usually done by an animal welfare organization, and certified farms are regularly inspected to ensure they are meeting the science-based standards.

certified organic—designation that tells consumers animals were raised without the use of antibiotics or added hormones and fed only organically grown feed. Certified farms must meet national organic standards.

cortisol—a hormone produced by the adrenal glands in animals (including humans) that helps the body respond to stress or danger by providing increased energy

deficiency—(in terms of diet) a shortage of the nutrients essential for good health

deforestation—the clearing or cutting down of forests by humans in order to produce wood products or create space for farming, grazing cattle or planting industrial crops. Global deforestation contributes to climate change and loss of animal species.

dissected—separated into pieces for examination, such as cutting open the body of a deceased animal or plant. Sometimes frogs, fetal pigs or other small animals are dissected in high school and university science classes so students can study their anatomical structure.

ecosystem—a biological community of interconnected and interdependent organisms in a certain region, such as a marine ecosystem, grassland ecosystem or forest ecosystem

exotic——introduced from another country or environment. Exotic animals suffer when they are taken from their natural habitats, and they can also harm the ecosystems they are brought to.

factory farms—large industrialized farms where large numbers of animals are raised in small indoor spaces in order to produce meat or other animal products quickly and cheaply

forage—wander in search of food (such as grass, leaves, berries, insects, etc.)

fossil fuels—materials found in the earth, such as oil, coal and natural gas, formed over millions of years from the fossilized remains of plants and animals. Burning fossil fuels releases gases like carbon dioxide, methane and nitrogen into the environment, which causes smog and contributes to climate change.

free run/free range—terms used to describe how chickens are raised. Free run means hens live uncaged inside barns and can freely move around. Most free run farms provide a private area for hens to lay their eggs, and some also provide perching areas. Free range hens live the same way but are allowed access to outside space (weather permitting).

grass finished—label for beef from cattle who have eaten nothing but grass their entire lives. (Grass fed refers to beef from cattle who started on a grass diet and were then switched to a grain-based diet the last few months of their lives.) Grass is preferable to grain, because grain gives cows a stomachache.

lactose intolerant—unable to fully digest lactose, a sugar found in milk and milk products, because the body is not producing the lactase enzyme that breaks down lactose. Drinking or eating milk products can cause a person with lactose intolerance to have stomach cramps, gas, and sometimes diarrhea or nausea. Cats and dogs who are lactose intolerant experience similar symptoms.

nervous system—the part of the body that coordinates behavior and transmits sensory information to and from various parts of the body. It includes the brain, spinal cord and the complex network of nerves that carry the information.

neutering—surgically removing a male animal's testicles so the animal can't reproduce (also called *castrating*). Removing a female animal's ovaries and uterus so she can't get pregnant is called *spaying*.

pandemic—an outbreak of an infectious disease (such as the flu) that occurs over a wide geographic area, affecting a large number of people across a country or worldwide

pangolin—a shy, nocturnal, insect-eating animal with scaly armor who lives in Asia and Africa. Pangolins are endangered due to being killed for their meat and scales, which are used in traditional Chinese medicine.

rights—the legal, social or ethical concepts of freedom or entitlement. International law says that all people have the right to have their basic human needs met. These include food, healthcare and education. Animal rights advocates believe that animals have similar basic rights and are entitled to live free from being used for food, clothing, labor, entertainment or medical testing, or being kept in captivity for any reason. In comparison, animal welfare advocates base their arguments for improving the treatment of animals on what science tells us about animal needs, rather than on the concept of rights.

salmonella—bacteria that affect the intestinal tract (also known as the digestive system) and make people and animals sick. Salmonella are spread through eating or drinking contaminated food or water, or handling infected animals and their food or toys. (You should wash your hands after touching pets and their supplies and after touching farm animals or wild animals such as turtles.)

thermoregulate—to regulate or maintain one's body temperature by changing position or behavior in relationship to physical surroundings (for example, using shade or water to cool off, or lying in the sun to store heat)

unethical—not conforming to the moral principles (ethics) that guide a person or community

urbanization—the process of land being taken over by expanding cities and towns

vaccination—the injection of a medicine (vaccine) that prevents an infectious disease caused by a virus or bacteria. A vaccine is introduced to the body to stimulate the body's immune system to recognize and fight that disease.

veterinary—relating to the science and practice of preventing or treating nonhuman animal diseases and injuries. A veterinarian ("vet" for short) is a doctor trained in veterinary medicine. Vets usually work in veterinary clinics or animal hospitals.

vitamin C—a vital nutrient found in various foods (especially fruits). It is also sold as a supplement. The body needs vitamin C. It can prevent scurvy (a disease people and animals get when they don't eat enough fruit) and can even help fight the common cold.

zoochosis—stress-related abnormal repetitive behavior with no apparent goal or function, seen in animals in zoos and other forms of captivity. Signs of distress include pacing, excessive licking, bar biting and overgrooming.

RESOURCES

Print

BC SPCA. *Bark!* The official magazine of the BC SPCA Kids Club, published quarterly in Burnaby, BC, by Canada Wide Media Limited.

Eriksson, Ann. *Bird's-Eye View: Keeping Wild Birds in Flight.* Victoria, BC: Orca Book Publishers, 2020.

Groc, Isabelle. *Gone Is Gone: Wildlife Under Threat.* Victoria, BC: Orca Book Publishers, 2019.

Laidlaw, Rob. *No Shelter Here: Making the World a Kinder Place for Dogs.* Toronto, ON: Pajama Press, 2011.

Laidlaw, Rob. *The Dog Patrol: Our Canine Companions and the Kids Who Protect Them.* Toronto, ON: Pajama Press, 2020.

Laidlaw, Rob. *Wild Animals in Captivity.* Markham, ON: Fitzhenry & Whiteside, 2008.

Suzuki, David, and Kathy Vanderlinden. *You Are the Earth: Know Your World So You Can Help Make It Better.* New York, NY: Greystone Books, 2012.

Weil, Zoe. *So, You Love Animals: An Action-Packed, Fun-Filled Book to Help Kids Help Animals.* Gabriola Island, BC: New Society Publishers, 2004.

Online

American Society for the Prevention of Cruelty to Animals (ASPCA): aspca.org

British Columbia Society for the Prevention of Cruelty to Animals (BC SPCA): spca.bc.ca (The BC SPCA also has a British Columbia province-wide hotline people can call to report an animal in distress: 1-855-622-7722.)

David Suzuki Foundation (wildlife and environment): davidsuzuki.org

Find the Birds (mobile bird-identification game being developed by Adam Dhalla): findthebirds.com

The Humane Society of the United States: humanesociety.org

iNaturalist app: apps.apple.com/us/app/inaturalist/id421397028

Nature Canada (wildlife): naturecanada.ca

World Animal Protection (worldwide animal issues): worldanimalprotection.org

Links to external resources are for personal and/or educational use only and are provided in good faith without any express or implied warranty. There is no guarantee given as to the accuracy or currency of any individual item. The author and publisher provide links as a service to readers. This does not imply any endorsement by the author or publisher of any of the content accessed through these links.

ERNIE PACHOLUK

ACKNOWLEDGMENTS

I would like to thank Craig Naherniak, general manager of humane education at the British Columbia Society for the Prevention of Cruelty to Animals (BC SPCA) and Meghann Cant, manager of companion animal welfare at the BC SPCA, for their careful review of and feedback on the content of this book. Thanks also to the BC SPCA for the use of many photographs and references from *Bark!*, the magazine of the BC SPCA Kids Club. My gratitude also goes to photographer Jo-Anne McArthur of We Animals Media and everyone else who shared photographs and information about their work with animals, and to Kirstie Hudson, my editor at Orca, who was a great help in honing this manuscript.

INDEX

*Page numbers in **bold** indicate an image caption.*

JACQUELINE PEARCE is the author of 12 books for children and teens. Her novels and nonfiction explore her fascination with local history, people, nature and animals, including *Dog House Blues* and *The Truth About Rats*, which were written for the BC SPCA Kids Club. Jacqueline has degrees in English literature and environmental studies. She has volunteered for the BC SPCA humane education program for many years and has both fostered and adopted many rescued animals with her family. She currently lives near Vancouver, British Columbia, with her husband, daughter, dog and two cats.

ORCA Think
Stay Curious!

Jen Sookfong Lee

FINDING HOME
The Journey of Immigrants and Refugees

ILLUSTRATED BY
Drew Shannon

SHELTER
Homelessness in Our Community

Lois Peterson
illustrated by Taryn Gee

WHAT'S THE BIG IDEA?

The Orca Think series introduces us to the issues making headlines in the world today. It encourages us to question, connect and take action for a better future. With those tools we can all become better citizens. Now that's smart thinking!

ORCA